Battlefield Afghanistan

AUTHOR'S APPEAL

As the global fight against terrorism continues, many brave countrymen of ours are being lost in the fight for our freedom and way of life.

In light of this, a percentage of the royalties from this book is being donated to the Special Forces Welfare Foundation, an organization that supports the families of those who have lost a loved one.

If you would like to help the foundation in its work, or make a donation, please write to:

> Special Forces Welfare Foundation
> Avpro Aerospace
> PO Box 9128
> Bollo Lane
> Acton
> London
> W3 6GE
> UK

Other charities I actively support include:

> www.mag.org.uk
> www.ssafa.org.uk
> www.armybenfund.org

Your kindness and generosity is greatly appreciated by all concerned.

Sincerely,

Mike Ryan

BATTLEFIELD AFGHANISTAN

by
Mike Ryan

SPELLMOUNT

British Library Cataloguing in Publication Data:
A catalogue record for this book is available
from the British Library

Copyright © Mike Ryan 2007

ISBN: 978-1-86227-390-0

First published in the UK in 2007 by
Spellmount Limited
The Mill, Brimscombe Port
Stroud, Gloucestershire GL5 2QG

Tel: 01453 883300
Fax: 01453 883233
Website: www.spellmount.com

1 3 5 7 9 8 6 4 2

Printed in Great Britain by
Oaklands Book Services
Stonehouse, Gloucestershire GL10 3RQ

Contents

Dedication

This book is dedicated to all the brave men and women of the armed forces who are fighting heroically for a brighter future for the long-suffering people of Afghanistan. Their selfless acts and professionalism are an inspiration to us all.

Acknowledgements

I would like to thank the following individuals, organizations and companies for their kind help in supporting me with the production of this book:

Shaun Barrington of Spellmount Publishing for believing in the book, Peter Robinson MA, John Ryan, Mark Bennis, The Major, Jackhammer, Dr John, Swampy, Dangerous Dale, BCMH, UK MoD, US Department of Defense, Australian Department of Defence, 16 AAB, 131 CDO, 45 CDO, The Firm, Household Cavalry, USMC, 160th SOAR, USAF SOG, NARA, DVIC and Avpro Aerospace.

Thanks also to my wife, Fiona and children, Isabella, Angelina and Jamie for their patience during my time away interviewing and researching for this book.

Photo credits: UK Ministry of Defence, Australian Department of Defence, Canadian Department of Defence, US Department of Defense, New Zealand Ministry of Defence, Avpro Aerospace, RAWA, CIA, SOCOM, USAF, US Marines, US Army, 3 Para, Royal Marines, Royal Navy, RAF, NARA, the White House, DVIC and anyone else who has kindly donated imagery for this book. Front cover: FPFI, European Press Photo Agency. Every effort has been made to acknowledge copyright in the images. If any omission has been committed, the publishers apologise and undertake to correct on reprint.

Author's Note

For operational security (OPSEC) reasons, certain technical, tactical, operational and procedural details have either been changed or omitted. This has been done deliberately for the protection and welfare of both our armed forces and those of our allies, as ongoing military operations are taking place in this region, and are likely to do so for years to come.

Preface

As I write this book, British Forces serving in Afghanistan are engaged in some of the fiercest and most vicious fighting experienced in any UK military operation since the Korean War in the 1950s. And yet, we are told by our politicians that they are on nothing more than a peace keeping mission that has come up against some unexpected resistance.

Nobody however, appears to have informed the opposition, the Taliban. They have turned to what the historian Michael Howard describes in his book *Empires, Nations and Wars* as 'the strategy of despair: terrorism'. They see the battlefields of Afghanistan as a Jihad against those who do not practise or believe in their values and their extreme interpretation of the Islamic faith.

For them, Afghanistan is merely a setting for their war of terror. For the West, it looks like a simple choice. Fight them in their own backyard and defeat them, or risk another franchise of Terror Inc getting stronger and more capable than it already is, creating a deadly platform for, potentially, some kind of Armageddon.

This book is not a comprehensive history of the warfare that has raged in Afghanistan over the centuries, nor indeed is it an account of every single battle, skirmish, firefight or contact that has taken place even in recent times. It is merely a snapshot of a moment in time in Afghanistan's turbulent history, which will fade for the many quickly, as they go about their daily lives, yet will live in the hearts and minds of the few that have fought there, forever.

Abbreviations

AAA	Anti-Aircraft Artillery
ANA	Afghan National Army
APC	Armoured Personnel Carrier
ATGM	Anti-Tank Guided Missile
ATGW	Anti-Tank Guided Weapon
CAS	Close Air Support
CIA	Central Intelligence Agency
C2	Command and Control
EXINT	Extraction/Insertion
FAC	Forward Air Controller
FOO	Forward Observation Officer
GPMG	General Purpose Machine-Gun
GRIT	Group Range Indication Target
HMG	Heavy Machine-Gun
IED	Improvised Explosive Device
IR	Infra-Red
JDAM	Joint Direct Attack Munition
JTAC	Joint Terminal Air Controller
LMG	Light Machine-Gun
LSW	Light Support Weapon
MANPADS	Man Portable Air Defence System
NATO	North Atlantic Treaty Organization
OEF	Operation Enduring Freedom
OPSEC	Operational Security
OPTAG	Operational Training Advisory Group
PVCP	Permanent Vehicle Check Point

SAM	Surface Air Missile
SAS	Special Air Service
SASR	Special Air Service Regiment (Australia)
SAW	Squad Assault Weapon
SBS	Special Boat Service
SEAL	Sea Air Land
SF	Special Forces
SOG	Special Operations Group
TAB	Tactical Advance to Battle
TAC	Air Tactical Air Support
UAV	Unmanned Air Vehicle

British SAS operative in Afghanistan.

Introduction

Afghanistan has been the graveyard for many, and provided salvation for few – yet they still keep coming. Why? Because this beautiful yet troubled landlocked country is of immense strategic importance – a fact not lost on its many invaders, including Alexander the Great, the British, the Russians, and more recently the Americans, following 9/11.

Although many have come, none as yet has conquered, nor indeed is it likely that any ever will, as Afghanistan's complicated tribal make-up, as well as its difficult geography, make life extremely difficult for any outsider to dominate and rule. Afghanistan, in essence, has always been a varied collection of tribes and immigrants, over whom there has been little or no central governmental control, and those that have been deemed successful have achieved only moderate influence.

To understand the challenges our armed forces face today, both politically and militarily, it is important to know something of Afghanistan's turbulent history, and indeed, its tribal make-up. There are three dominant languages spoken, with numerous minority languages also to contend with. The country is overwhelmingly Islamic, but its community is sub-divided among Hanafi Sunnis, Inmami Shia, Ismailis Shia, and Sufis. The geography of the land varies immensely, from desert to high mountain, which makes for difficult and vulnerable communication systems. Those that do exist – primarily highway and trail based – link up at various points around the major towns and cities, creating a crude but workable method of getting about. Surprisingly, there is no railway network as yet, which seems odd, considering the fact that two of Afghanistan's invaders, Britain and Russia, are both great fans of railway-based transportation systems. One can only assume that their construction and operation was deemed too difficult during their respective periods of occupation.

For those in the West, the Afghan tribal system is hard to comprehend logically; they seem to fight amongst themselves all the time. And yet, as soon as an invader arrives, you guessed it, they unite, fight them, and then revert back to their old ways. Most of these feuds stem from tribal, religious, or ethnic blood disagreements; but occasionally they are over money, as security and protection is big business in Afghanistan these days.

The current tactic employed by the West in Afghanistan is to pay tribal leaders for their support in the ongoing fight against the Taliban. But many have long memories of their suffering under former occupation, and are holding back until a clear winner emerges. On occasions a compromise is reached, where the tribal leaders agree to be impartial and to stay out of the fighting altogether, which at times is quite an achievement. Personally, I fundamentally disagree with the policy of paying tribal leaders for providing security in their own regions: at best, it encourages corruption, and at worst, it exacerbates the security problem, as some tribes have been known to attack their own people as a means of creating more instability, leading to ever greater demands for money for supposed further security enhancements. For good reason, the Americans call this policy 'the self-licking ice-cream'. A better way would be to pay them for the level of peace preserved, as that would have a more calming effect on the region and would speed the reconstruction process. This is, in fact, critical, as a major cornerstone of the 'hearts and minds' policy that is needed to win over the Afghan people. You may think I am being cynical and pessimistic. I am not, I am merely an optimist with experience. As for the Afghans, they have every right to be wary of occupiers, and it is understandable that they view every move we currently make with scepticism. For we British have been the most frequent of visitors to Afghanistan – and the memory of our long and varied time spent in this country is very much alive.

THE GREAT GAME

Our first incursion took place in 1839, and was brought about after Moscow showed interest in Afghanistan, seeing it as part of its future Central Asian empire. Russian expansionism in Central Asia had first begun as early as 1734, and its clear desire to have Afghanistan under its wing had became obvious to the British by the late 1830s. Thus a power struggle took place between the British and the Russians, often described as the Great Game. This was played out along the unsettled northern frontier of British India, and what land lay between Russia and India itself. That contested region happened to be in Afghanistan. A showdown between the empire of the Russian Bear and that of the British Bulldog looked inevitable. The Russians described their motives for operations in the region as to establish law and order along their southern border, as well as to abolish slave trading, prevalent in the area at the time. The British, however, felt that the Russians were trying to weaken their power base so as to gain access to a warm water port. Officially, the party line was that they were defending the frontiers of British India. Eventually, British forces invaded and began what was the First Anglo-Afghan War (1839–1842).The British claimed that they had invaded as a counter to Russian influence, and after several years of hard fighting they withdrew. With the British out of Afghanistan, the Russians continued with their empire expansion plans, and by 1869 they had reached the Amu Daryu (Oxus) river on the northern Afghan border.

This caused the British serious concern, but they stayed out of the country until as late as 1878, when they invaded again, the Second Anglo-Afghan War. The spark this time was the arrival of a Russian diplomatic mission to Kabul. After the British withdrew, relations between the two empires slowly improved, leading to the Anglo-Russian Treaty of 1907. The Russians agreed that Afghanistan lay outside its sphere of influence and that in future it would confer with Britain vis-à-vis its interests within the country. In return, Britain agreed not to interfere with the internal affairs of the country, specifically promising not to annex or occupy it in any way. Although the British and the Russians honoured the terms of the Treaty, the Amir of Afghanistan refused to recognize it, and following an incident perpetrated by his soldiers in British India in 1919, the third Anglo-Afghan War started. This time the impetus came from an Afghan border incursion, in which troops loyal to the Amir had seized a village and attempted a local revolt. The response from the British was swift: invasion and further conflict.

A NEW RED DAWN

During this short war, the Afghan government asked for Russian military aid, but it ended before any could be provided. The request, however, started a new relationship with the Russian Bolshevik government, so something good apparently came of something bad.

Eventually a political settlement was reached with Britain, in which Afghanistan gained full independence from its occupiers. This was a blessing at the time for all concerned, especially so for Afghanistan, as it was to enjoy a rare period of relative peace. That was until Russia decided to begin the Afghan game afresh. At first it was just a case of sponsoring maverick groups within the region – such as the Congress of the East in Baku – who called for a holy war against British imperialism. Then it was economic and military aid; always a good card to play when you want to get a foothold in a

The rusting remains of Soviet trucks in Afghanistan.

country, as you then have a marker that you can call in at any given time. This tends to create a puppet government – a favourite status quo with Russian political players. In 1929, one of the puppets, Amin Amanullah, was overthrown, leaving Russia's strategic position exposed. To rectify the situation, Russia sent in a force of 1,000 military personnel, who, disguised as Afghans, tried to restore him to power. Unfortunately for them, international condemnation forced them to withdraw, leaving their investment vulnerable once again. Although Britain and Russia were not at war during this period, they still vied for advantage and influence over the region, creating a political power vacuum in Afghanistan once the British had withdrawn from India and Pakistan in 1947.

After the death of Stalin, Russia stepped up its interest in Afghanistan, mainly through the supply of armaments and economic aid. They also helped bring Afghanistan into the modern age, through aid projects, building hospitals, airfields, hydro-electric dams, and the spectacular Salang Pass tunnel. By 1963, Soviet military advisers were deployed throughout Afghanistan in large numbers, with Afghan Officers undergoing their training in the USSR. In 1978, a small group of Soviet-trained Afghan officers seized control of the government and declared the foundation of a state with the laughably inappropriate new name of the Democratic Republic of Afghanistan; which was in essence a puppet state of the Soviet Union. As a result, civil war broke out throughout Afghanistan.

... with the present quality of our troops [in Afghanistan] I feel no confidence in their succeeding in such difficult country against an elusive enemy. Hence I think we should try any expedient which can obviate military operations. Untrammelled action from the air seems to offer the best hope.

Sir Hamilton Grant to Lord Chelmsford,
on operations in the Tochi Valley, 1919

I

Baiting the Bears

To understand and fully appreciate the current position of our forces in Afghanistan, it is instructive to know something of the Russian experience during their occupation of this extraordinary country in the 1980s. In fact, from a military perspective, it is imperative: lessons learned from the shedding of their blood yesterday will save that of our soldiers today. Why? Because the armed forces of the then Soviet Union were immense and powerful, and yet they lost. They had armour, attack aircraft, bombers, helicopters, special forces and a massive conventional army. On paper at least, it should have been a cake-walk. For the Russians, Afghanistan was their Vietnam. The political and military fall-out of their bitter experience in the 1980s lives on to this day. For them, it all started to go wrong in 1979 – when they made the fatal decision to invade.

The Soviet invasion of Afghanistan stemmed from a desire to control – following the disastrous reaction of the Afghan people to the new Democratic Republic of Afghanistan government – the destiny of a new socialist state, governed by a communist party. The Soviets felt that they had no choice but to come to the aid of the new government and felt compelled to act immediately. The need for quick, robust action was urgent because the state only controlled some of the cities, and even there, the position was parlous. Outside the cities, it was the tribal elders and clan chiefs who ran the

1

Russian BTRs form up in convoy prior to an operation in Afghanistan.

countryside; and sensing that their new government was totally ineffective, they quickly exploited the situation to their own advantage. The primary reason for this government's failure was simple. They were split down the middle, and were so engrossed with infighting that they took their eye off the ball, stalling the very purpose of their mission: the spreading of the gospel of socialism. Worse still, their message of creating a new egalitarian society by means of equal land distribution, the emancipation of women and the sweeping away of traditional Afghan values found little support amongst the Islamic tribes. Ironically, the only good thing to come from this government was the fact that they were so hated by the Afghan people that they actually succeeded in galvanizing all the factions and power bases at the same time, bringing them together, a feat that nobody else had managed in centuries. The final straw came when the President of Afghanistan was murdered by his prime minister, an illustration, if any were needed, of how bad the faction fighting had become. (Now *that's* political infighting.) The prime minister quickly became the new president, but was worse than the previous one, which is saying something. The army mutinied, law and order broke down, and villages and cities revolted, culminating in civil war.

THE SOVIET INVASION

It was 1979, and the Soviet General Secretary Leonard Brezhnev had seen enough. He decided to act before his client state of Afghanistan disintegrated before his very eyes. He gathered his General Staff together, and they recommended using the intervention model that was used in Hungary in 1956 and Czechoslovakia in 1968, but with some variations. Their plans however, were seriously flawed; as they were to discover later in the mission phase. The key truth that had been overlooked was that Afghanistan was embroiled in an all-out civil war: so a *coup de main* would only take control of the central government, and not that of the mainly rural population. Thus the intervention was doomed from the very start.

To the Soviet Union's credit militarily, the initial invasion of Afghanistan went extremely well, especially so as many of the participating units were only briefed days before the Christmas Eve commencement of the operation. The military invasion itself was masterfully planned, and well executed and the seizure of the government and termination of the president's authority were quickly accomplished. Within days, the Russians had their own president in place and quickly set about the business of restoring order. Their plan was three-fold: to restore order nationally by means of the Democratic Republic Army; to strengthen and restructure it for long-term stability; and then withdraw their own support forces after three years. However, there was one insuperable problem: the Democratic Republic Army was broken and totally dispirited, and in no position to suppress an all-out revolt.

For the Russians, losing face is everything and the thought of a total defeat was just too much to contemplate. But this was the most likely scenario, once they withdrew their own forces. To put this situation into context, one must remember the Russian psyche for warfare, which during the 1980s was geared up and trained for fighting large-scale, high tempo operations, and not guerrilla warfare. It is indeed most odd that it never occurred to them that they may one day face the same nightmare that the Americans had faced in Vietnam – and possibly even the same fate! Like a lumbering giant, they were slow to react to the unpredictability of unconventional warfare, and paid a heavy price for that failure. This is in contrast to the British Army in Afghanistan today, which trains and fights at section level – and gives a lot of tactical and command autonomy to its junior ranking soldiers – making them far better equipped to fight small groups or individuals. The Russians were at the time just the opposite, constrained by the need to refer every significant decision up the chain of command for approval.

Further complicating the situation for them was the long and convoluted process of making a decision, even when the situation had been sent up the chain, as there was no one person who could take a view on anything. Instead, everything had to be agreed by a committee of the collective leadership that had been put in charge, following General Secretary Brezhnev's severe decline in health in 1980. This sorry state of affairs went on until his death in 1982 – only to be repeated when he was succeeded by Yuri Andropov, who barely lasted two years in the post.

At this time, the Russian military leadership was recommending withdrawal, as they could see the writing was on the wall, but alas, their political masters could not. A situation not too dissimilar to ours today, vis-à-vis our involvement in Iraq. By 1984, the situation in Afghanistan was desperate, yet the politicians refused to budge. (During this period, the Soviet Union's General Secretary was Konstantin Chernenko, but

Russian Spetsnaz prepare for a mission.

like his predecessors he didn't last long in the job, as he died in 1985.) The final closure for Russia in Afghanistan eventually came about after Mikhail Gorbachev came to power. Prior to his arrival, the attitude was basically plod on and let's see what happens. But Gorbachev wanted a conclusion – one way or the other. Instinctively, his first thought was to increase the tempo of operation and thus Russia had the bloodiest year of the war so far: a situation not a million miles away from what is happening in Afghanistan and Iraq in 2007.

Unlike his former Politburo mates, Gorbachev was a realist, and it farly quickly dawned on him that there was no victory for Russia in Afghanistan, with the current military strategy; and anything more drastic risked alienating him on the world stage. His only way forward now, was to order a withdrawal; and a dignified avenue for this to be carried out was provided courtesy of the United Nations. By mutual agreement, half of the Soviet military force in Afghanistan had withdrawn by October 1988 and a steady draw-down continued until the last element of this once mighty military beast returned to Russian soil on 15 February 1989.

Soviet T-55s sit rusting near Bagram air base.

Insurgents' arms. A happy sixtieth to the AK-47, according to Amnesty International, 'the world's worst regulated firearm'. Something of an understatement.

If a man fears death, he will accept fever – Afghan proverb

LEARNING THE LESSONS

It would be very easy to dismiss the Russian experience in Afghanistan, as being irrelevant to that being endured by our forces today – but foolish. Why? Because in many cases, the Taliban are using virtually the same tactics, weapons, equipment – even the same kill zones – as those used by the Mujahideen againt the Russians. Our forces are taking casualties in regions of Afghanistan where, if only the lessons of the Russian experience were studied and learned, those losses could be reduced significantly or even eradicated. The Afghans are creatures of habit, and an ambush site that was good enough for use by the Mujahideen against the Russians in the past is still basically deemed good enough for use by the Taliban against us now – and that is their Achilles' heel. The sheer fact that they are predictable in many ways makes them vulnerable, so we need to be more pro-active in Afghanistan, rather than reactive. That way, we can use their tactics as a weapon against them. Contrary to popular belief, there were Russian strategists and tacticians who realised this also, but by the time they did, it was too late, as they had already lost the 'hearts and minds' battle with the Afghan people. And to win in guerrilla warfare, you must have the population at large on your side.

Where and why, did it all go so wrong for the Russians in Afghanistan? It is a question that has long been debated by 'Armchair Generals' the world over. On Christmas Eve 1979, when most of the world was relaxing and in festive spirit, who would have thought of invading another country? The

Russians of course – and with deadly effect. On that night, the sky above Kabul suddenly filled with Soviet aircraft, and within a five-hour period they had landed and secured its airport, paving the way for a massive airlift involving some 280 transport aircraft. Packed with assault troops and equipment, the Il-76, An-22 and An 12 aircraft quickly deposited their loads and left, as a further 100 aircraft carrying elements of the 103rd, 104th and 105th Airborne were on their way. They knew that there would be little military threat or resistance initially, as both the KGB and Russia's elite Spetsnaz units had anticipated them all in advance of the invasion phase – and indeed neutralized them. One classic and simple ploy they used countered the Afghan Army's tanks and armoured personnel carriers. Realizing that these vehicles posed quite a significant threat, the Russians sent out a recall notice stating that they were all required back in their MT sheds for modifications. The Afghans fell for the ruse, and as a result were in no position to fight back effectively against such a formidable force. With no serious opposition, the Russians quickly set about dividing the country into two separate military districts, both of which had armour, helicopter and air assets. It was clear that the Russians must have rehearsed their invasion plan punctiliously in advance, as there were no serious glitches during the initial phase. It has always been speculated that rehearsals took place in both South Yemen and Ethiopia for this operation, and that some lessons were learned for many other scenarios that would be encountered in Afghanistan. But it would seem guerrilla warfare was not one of them.

Prior to the invasion, the Russians had planned on using some of the 80,000 members of the Afghan Army as a surrogate force to secure the countryside; but with low morale, and no faith in the communist cause, many left legitimately or deserted, leaving the Army with barely 30,000 usable troops. Even those who stayed had loyalties elsewhere, as they often

Guerrilla fighter with RPG 1. This features a fragmenation warhead.

tipped the tribal leaders off about forthcoming operations, especially so if they were of the same clan. The Russians also frequently and inadvertently gave away their intentions in future operations, through their elaborate field inspections and vehicle parades. The Mujahideen quickly learned that when these took place, something was in the air, giving them either the option of a pre-emptive attack, or if the force was too large, time to withdraw.

In terms of guerrilla activity in Afghanistan, during the Soviet occupation no accurate numbers are available, but the generally accepted figure is that between 85,000 to 100,000 freedom fighters were active. This, compared to the Soviets, who fielded 140,000 troops in-country and a further 30,000 in support on the Soviet border with Afghanistan, is a substantial figure. You will have noticed that I have chosen to use the word freedom fighter. This is deliberate, as the Afghan people saw themselves as victims of an army of occupation and the term 'Mujahideen fighter' was often used by the Afghan people when describing a person who fights for the removal of an unwanted invader. This term is not accurate when describing the Taliban in Afghanistan, as they are invaders themselves, and are most certainly not engaged in fighting for the freedom of the Afghan people.

The Mujahideen themselves were often made up of former members of the Afghan Army – who by definition were trained fighters. This was particularly useful to the cause, as they were already savvy with Russian operational tactics, and there-fore could counter-act them. Where possible, the Mujahideen tried to set ambushes in areas with which they were both familiar and comfortable, as there was far more chance of a successful outcome. Prior to the arrival of Afghan Army deserters, the Mujahideen had been largely composed of local residents who took up arms together, and often embarked on ad hoc raids against local district capital armouries for their weaponry. Initially, their weapons ranged from swords to muskets and British bolt-action rifles formerly supplied to Afghanistan. Although old, they were highly prized, as they were far more accurate at long range than the Russian AK-47 assault rifle. Generally, the leaders of the guerrilla forces came from local villages, with few having had any formal mili-tary training. During the early days of the revolt, resistance was organized along ethnic and tribal lines, with very few coordinated attacks taking place. However, Afghanistan's neighbours, Iran and Pakistan, soon came to their aid, as they themselves feared Soviet invasion. Eventually, other countries such as the USA, the People's Republic of China, Britain, France, Italy, Saudi Arabia, and Egypt began provid-ing humanitarian, financial and military assistance as well, this being done mainly through Pakistan. Military training was covertly provided by some of the countries named. As may be imagined, much of this activity was classified at the time, and in some cases, it still is. The CIA, for instance, had a major support mission in Afghanistan , providing everything from Stinger Surface-to-air missiles (MANPADS) to covert operatives: some of whom trained Osama bin Laden. At one stage, they even engaged in operations directly, when they used precision guided mortar rounds against Russian defensive positions. The UK was involved through the SAS, who provided both direct and indirect support. At one stage, they were even training Mujahideen fighters in Scotland, until a farmer spotted them running around his land, and thinking they were illegal immigrants, called the police. Needless to say, they were covertly flown out of the country within hours of their discovery.

For the Americans, this whole chapter in Afghanistan's history is extremely controversial, and is coming back to haunt them. Many of Al-Qaeda's most effective and dangerous terrorists were financed, equipped and trained by them. As they say, 'Never keep somebody else's wild dog in your own backyard, as it could turn and bite your ass.' The Americans, are not the only ones with Mujahideen issues that are haunting them.

Pakistan is hurting also, their pain derived from the Taliban, rather than the Mujahideen, as they were the father of this bastard son. As mentioned, Pakistan, of course, had its own motives for acting as a supply hub to Afghanistan, the main one being its fear that it too could fall victim to Soviet occupation. Their fears were heightened by the Russians frequently bombing inside Pakistan borders. This was often done for tactical reasons, but on occasions it served as a warning shot to Pakistan to basically mind its own business. Pakistan's Inter-Services Intelligence Agency (ISI) was the administrator for aid to the Mujahideen. It was also the creator of the Taliban. The ISI were experts in manipulation, able to manage the various Afghan political factions that were headquartered in Pakistan by means of canalising the aid, sometimes damming it up.

The main seven factions were determined by their tribal leader's religious convictions and were split between three which were Islamic moderates and four which were Islamic fundamentalists. To gain aid, the ISI required all the various ethnic and tribal Mujahideen groups operating in Afghanistan to join one of their nominated factions. Needless to say, the favoured factions grew in political power and were in key positions to exploit the post-communist power struggle that took place once the Soviets had been put to flight. Essentially, the more fundamentalist you were – the more aid you got. As most Mujahideen fighters were unpaid volunteers, any aid they received (or war spoils they took) made a lot of difference to both them and their families.

As the war gained momentum, new, mobile Mujahideen units emerged from within the factions. These units were made up of mainly single men, who were well trained and motivated compared to the other conventional units. They were also, tactically, more valuable, as they could cover greater distances, making them a crude but effective force multiplier. From the earliest days of the Afghan-Soviet war, it became clear that the strategic centre of gravity of this war was logistics. Basically, he who destroyed the opponents supply chain was going to win. It makes perfect sense, as everything from fuel to food and arms to ammunition has to use a highway or track at some point. This point of weakness was more vulnerable for the Soviets, as they had a massive mechanized army to support, whereas the Mujahideen generally only had animals, or the odd 4x4 pick-up truck at their disposal. Of the two, the Russians were hit hardest, as they were continually ambushed along their long lines of communication, on occasions more than once during a single supply trip. As a counter-measure, they set about dropping millions of anti-personnel mines along road verges and hill tops, intending to maim or kill the Mujahideen fighters as they moved into potential ambush points. This tactic had limited success, as the guerrilla fighters often sent animals over their designated ambush points first, or on occasions, captured prisoners!

Russian SU-25, NATO codename: Frog Foot.

Mines are totally indiscriminate and hurt both friend and foe alike. The Russians, however, liked them, and made great use of all kinds – especially the smaller plastic types. They even went so far as manufacturing some to resemble children's toys, as these would be brought back to the parents, causing injuries to a whole family rather than an individual. The Russian philosophy on mine warfare was this. Kill one Mujahideen fighter and that's one out of the fight. But injure one, and it's five you take out of the fight, as four others have to carry him. Other uses for mines included the protecting of Soviet bases, the sealing of escape routes, and the isolation of possible Mujahideen villages. The Russians also used chemical warfare, but its use was restricted to remote areas where access was either too difficult or deemed too risky for conventional insertion. They used many different agents, but one favourite was a tar-like substance that burst into flames on contact with human flesh or the tyres of a vehicle. This substance probably contained phosphorous, which bursts into flames once in contact with air. Again, most victims of this type of weapon were children. The Soviet tactics were designed to eliminate support for the Mujahideen in rural areas, but generally they had the opposite effect. In addition to the heavy use of mines, they often bombed farms and rural villages, destroyed crops and water irrigation systems, and even slaughtered animal herds en masse as a means of denying food to the fighters and their familes. They were drawing an inference from Mao Tse Tung's dictum that the guerrilla lives in the population like a fish in water. They tried to kill off the fish by draining the water away.

This strategy caused a massive humanitarian crisis, as over seven million rural inhabitants were forced to flee Afghanistan for other countries, mainly Pakistan and Iran. In part this approach worked, as the Mujahideen were forced to rely on foreign aid or captured Russian supplies for survival. But this of course meant that they had to mount even more attacks on the Russians, so in this reaction the strategy was counter-productive. A second reaction was that the Mujahideen set up remote supply bases, which were usually located either underground or in caves. The Russians responded to this by mounting large scale 'sweep and clear operations' – which were very reminiscent of those mounted by the Americans in Vietnam. The Russian version of 'sweep and clear' was very similar to that of the Americans as they both favoured the use of helicopters. For the Mujahideen, however, helicopters meant targets – lots of them.

Here is a brief description of how an anti 'sweep and clear' ambush would be set. Generally, the Mujahideen would set up a false camp as a lure, then watch and wait until the bees came to the honey. Around the camp would be copious amounts of IEDs or mines, which were usually deployed under the anticipated LZ. Further out from the camp, they would set up kill zones with interlocking fields of fire. Weapons

Guerrilla fighters armed with RPG 2s. These feature anti-armour HEAT warheads, which are lethal against snatch Landrovers.

usually deployed consisted of RPGs, AK-47 assault rifles and heavy machine guns. The Mujahideen waited until the troop-carrying helicopters of the Russian force had either landed or flared before opening fire. They were in their most vulnerable position at this point and helicopters flying top cover for them could not fire for fear of hitting their own side. This complication was also further exploited by the Mujahideen advancing as close to the enemy as possible, in a bid to try and create the risk of a friendly fire situation. In general, these tactics worked extremely well for the Mujahideen; but there were times when they would withdraw, rather than engage. Withdrawal was usually the result of an instant tactical assessment. If for instance, the Russians had Mil-24 Hind helicopter gun-ships at their disposal, then the Mujahideen would be extremely wary of attacking, as these were armoured to withstand all but the heaviest calibre of round, and were very difficult to shoot down. They could be brought down

Mil-24 Hind helicopter.

by RPGs – but only by a lucky shot, as these were, and are, inaccurate at long range. Even the infamous US-supplied Stinger MANPADS had difficulty engaging and destroying these helicopters. The Mujahideen often called the Hind, 'The Devil's Chariot', as it was greatly feared on account of both its protection and deadly weapon systems . The Hind's armament usually comprised rockets, guided missiles, machine-guns and a 23mm nose mounted cannon. It also featured very sophisticated avionics that enabled all weather operations to be carried out by day or night. It was, perhaps, the Soviets' most effective weapon system in Afghanistan. Other weapons that the Mujahideen feared in the Soviet armoury included the ZSU-23-4, a Russian self-propelled air defence system that was radar guided and featured 4 x 23mm cannons that could be fired simultaneously to great effect. Although designed for air defence, the Soviets used them in Afghanistan for counter-ambush and precision ground attack – and as with the Hind, the Mujahideen were very cautious when dealing with a Russian force equipped with this system.

One particular tactic that the Russians used with great success against large groups of Mujahideen fighters was the 'Hammer and Anvil'. In this move, they identified a

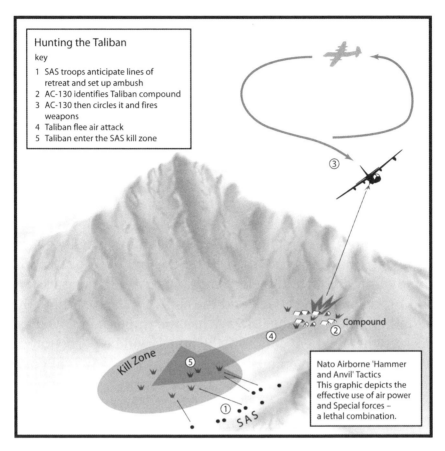

Hunting the Taliban

key

1 SAS troops anticipate lines of retreat and set up ambush
2 AC-130 identifies Taliban compound
3 AC-130 then circles it and fires weapons
4 Taliban flee air attack
5 Taliban enter the SAS kill zone

Compound

Kill Zone

Nato Airborne 'Hammer and Anvil' Tactics
This graphic depicts the effective use of air power and Special forces – a lethal combination.

SAS

Russian 'hammer and anvil' tactics proved highly effective against the Mujahideen, hence their continued use against the Taliban.

… the Soviets seem to lack an adequate quick-reaction airstrike capability in support of field troops. To receive an airstrike, a junior-grade infantry officer must send a request, which is forwarded up to the division level in the Army and then over to the Air Force; there are delays at each command level and communications point. … The compound communications structure tends to hamper support for truck convoys or airborne operations unless events proceed strictly in accordance with the advanced plan.

Lieutenant-Colonel Denny R. Nelson,
Air University Review, January–February 1985

Mujahideen compound, then bombed and strafed it until the fighters within were forced to flee. That's the Hammer part. The Anvil part is where the guerrilla fighters' anticipated escape routes were either mined or lined with ambushing forces, who then decimated them by means of overwhelming fire-power. When executed well, this tactic was simply devastating.

What most often took place between the Russians and the Mujahideen in Afghanistan was a game of cat and mouse that pitched small groups of relatively poorly armed men against numerically superior, well equipped forces; and yet more often than not, the small groups prevailed. In virtually every case that I have ever studied, three factors decide the outcome of an ambush: the element of surprise, the aggression and precision of the attack and the speed of its execution. By definition, the ambusher always has the upper hand, as they decide where, when, and how the attack will be perpetrated. For the victim of an ambush, the only way out is to fight your way out. And for every second you remain in the ambusher's kill zone, you may be taking casualties. These are standard tactics, and yet the Russians failed on many occasions to use them. They did, in fairness, get a lot sharper towards the end of their occupation – but at a cost. Not helping their situation was the heavy use of conscription. Just as their soldiers had become operationally adept and tactically useful, their two years was up. And the training cycle started all over again. Internal feuds within the army did not help: many Russian soldiers lost their lives because of them. In one particular example, two Russian officers were involved in a dispute over the affections of a female soldier, which led to one of them withholding vital intelligence information that led to the other's death, as well as those of his entire column. Other examples of Russian military failures against the Mujahideen include basic field discipline breakdowns; failing to post sentries, smoking in a tactical situation, talking while in ambush positions, failing to secure the high ground during ground offensives, failure to secure vulnerable choke points along convoy routes. As mentioned before, the Mujahideen regularly used inherited tribal ambush points against the Russians to inflict a 'death by a thousand cuts'. They did this against the British also during their occupation and guess what – the Taliban are still using the very same positions.

In summary, the Russians made a lot of mistakes in Afghanistan, but they also got a lot of things right. We need to encompass more of their positive experiences in our OPTAG training, as many lives could be saved; and indeed the demise of the Taliban could be brought about far quicker if only we heed the lessons.

Russian ZSU-23-4.

US General Tommy Franks with Special Forces.

II

Avenging Angels

Following the Soviet withdrawal from Afghanistan, the world seemingly lost interest in this country as it often did, but inside it was business as usual. The tribal leaders picked up their turf wars from where they last left them off, and the new kings of the hill, who had grown their territorial empires during the Afghan-Soviet War, battled to retain and expand their new kingdoms. In the north of Afghanistan, a collection of tribes – known to the media as the Northern Alliance – were deemed the good guys and thus benefited from some direct support from the United States. This support came mainly in the form of military advisers – both CIA and special forces – but in terms of money and military hardware, the aid was to all intents and purposes non existent.

The Alliance was led by a very popular and charismatic Commander, called Ahmad Shah Massoud, nicknamed the Lion of Panjshir. Massoud had risen to prominence during the Soviet invasion and was seen as a future leader of Afghanistan, on account of both his military and political skills, which were legendary within the country. He anticipated the growth of outside influence within Afghanistan and was a vocal critic of Pakistan, considering it a major threat to the region. To the outside world, Pakistan was seen as a conduit for aid to Afghanistan, and nothing more. But to Massoud they were another Soviet Union in-waiting, as he had seen how they were slowly taking over Afghanistan by way of their proxy

Ahmad Shah Massoud.

militant creation, the Taliban. He repeatedly warned the West of his concerns, but as usual, it all fell on deaf ears. His frustration was deepened by the fact that when he asked for military support to help thwart the Taliban's encroachment it was denied. The Americans were actually supporting the Taliban, albeit indirectly and unknowingly at first. This came about through the funding and aid that they were supplying to Pakistan for distribution to Afghanistan's refugee population – or so they thought! It was in fact being used to finance Pakistan's ambitions in Afghanistan. Massoud did not live to see his warnings or predictions come true, as he was assassinated just two days before the tragic events of 9/11. His death is thought to have been ordered by Osama bin Laden, Al-Qaeda's front man in Afghanistan, as Massoud was drawing too much attention to their movement. Massoud put it simply: 'The main scourge of our country is perennial foreign intervention ... only final cessation of foreign aggression will allow us to start solving all other problems of Afghanistan, economic and political.'

To illustrate his point, around this time, former Pakistani Prime Minister Benazir Bhutto admitted that Pakistan had been heavily involved in the creation of the Taliban, but insisted that there were others involved, including the UK and the USA, who, she alleges, supplied them with arms via Saudi Arabian finance. One must of course treat these comments with some caution; but Saudi Arabia is a known supporter and financier of Al-Qaeda and the possibility that it is still bank-rolling the Taliban today is intriguing. Pakistan also admits to providing training to the Pashtun Afghan refugees, who were originally the backbone of the Taliban prior to the large-scale introduction of foreign fighters to its ranks. The vast majority of these are of Pakistani origin. As for the Lion of Panjshir, his legacy lives on, named 'National Hero' of Afghanistan in 2002 by order of the current President, Hamid Karzai. If only he had been listened to, then arguably the terrible events of September 11, 2001 in the US might not have taken place.

This was no simple terrorist incident, it was a sophisticated, coordinated and sustained attack that clearly took a lot of meticulous planning and foresight. Naturally, the attack caused great embarrassment to the American Intelligence networks, as they had failed to stop it despite growing evidence that something was in the air. In hindsight, they had all the pieces of the intel picture, but just didn't know how it all fitted together. An attack on the US mainland had always been predicted, but nobody could have possibly imagined this one. Investigations quickly revealed that all four aircraft involved had been hijacked by Arab terrorists under the alleged leadership of America's arch enemy, Osama bin Laden. The attacks were extremely well executed, demonstrating to the world that this terrorist group was sophisticated and well

US Special Forces in Afghanistan on a building adorned with a poster of Massoud, known to his followers as Amer Sahib (Commander).

connected, and operated as part of a worldwide network. Only one terrorist group was capable of such a spectacular and indeed only one was in the frame from the beginning. That group was Al-Qaeda. 'Al-Qaeda' means literally 'the base', and its origins are in Saudi Arabia, where its leader, Osama bin Laden also hails from. On several occasions, America has tried to assassinate him – even resorting to cruise missiles at one stage – but to no avail, he is still at large. The view of the United States is that sooner or later they will get him, just like they did Saddam Hussein. But when that's going to be, nobody knows.

In the aftermath of 9/11, there was just one question on everyone's mind: what was America and her allies going to do about it? In this highly charged and emotional period in America's history, there were fears of a rash reaction by President George W. Bush, but to his credit, he remained remarkably composed and rational. But America really only had one course of action: retribution. And this, they set about extracting, and very quickly. So quickly in fact, that many were caught off-guard when reports began appearing in the press, the week after 9/11, alleging that British and American special forces were already engaging in running gun battles with the Taliban and Al-Qaeda. This proved to be an exaggeration, but what was abundantly clear was that something really was going down in Afghanistan, long before the official announcements of declared action. At that particular time, I personally was in a slightly awkward position, as I had just finished working with both the British and American special forces on a project that was totally unrelated to the 'War on Terror' yet gave me an insight into what was going on, through the simple fact that everyone I knew in this world was disappearing off the radar rapidly! E-mails stopped, phones went to answer-machine permanently, and wives and girlfriends of those I worked with were told abruptly that their loved ones were in isolation, and that they could have no direct contact with them for the time being: a living nightmare for them and their families, I can assure you. For me, the situation got even more complicated as I was constantly being tasked at this time with giving interviews to Sky, ITN and the BBC about what was going on; trying to walk a very thin line, giving an informed opinion while not compromising OPSEC. The first confirmation of US direct involvement in Afghanistan I saw was a TV broadcast showing footage of the Taliban dancing around an aircraft that they claimed to have just shot down. It was in fact a Gnat unmanned air vehicle (UAV), its owners being the CIA. For them, revenge could not come around quick enough, as they were being held responsible for the multiple intelligence failures that led to the terrorist attacks on 9/11, and this was payback time.

The CIA, to its credit, had put boots on the ground in Afghanistan within days of 9/11, the personnel involved mainly coming from the SOG (Special Operations Group). Their mission was to help kick-start the war against Terrorism Inc prior to the arrival of US conventional forces. This they did by means of that venerable US incentive. Dollars, and lots of them; millions in fact, all flown into Afghanistan in suitcases on board a rickety old Mil helicopter, left over from the Soviet–Afghan war of the 1980s. I met one of those involved in this operation in 2002, while visiting Washington DC. He must have been in his mid sixties – not quite what I would have expected – but it transpired that he spoke Farsi really well, and in his words they 'broke open the bottle' saying 'use in event of emergency only'. I'm sure he was being modest, as he struck me as a street-wise hombre who clearly knew his business. He described one of his covert flights into Indian country as an experience not to be missed.

The helicopter he was in had a wire coat hanger as a means of securing the door and oil leaked profusely from the engine gearbox above his head down onto him. He politely made the

'CIA Dave' was working with Mike Spann when he was killed; see p. 41.

pilot aware of his slight concern, only to be told that it was a good sign, as it meant that there was still some oil in the engine. Other craziness quickly followed, as they were operating out of a mud-built building in the middle of nowhere, with no place to store the money securely. This meant each person in the team taking turns to sleep on it for safekeeping. A great feeling I'm sure, if it was your own money – but not if it's Uncle Sam's. The CIA's new-found friends, the Northern Alliance, of course offered to guard it, but their offer was politely declined. Other interesting aspects of this venture include the use of an old, clapped-out radio system from the seventies for comms, as parts were still readily available in Afghanistan, plus the locals knew how to fix it. This contraption fed the daily intel picture back to the States for analysis prior to special forces deployment in support of the Northern Alliance. So as to make sure it was all being taken seriously

A CIA spook from the Special Activities Division.

back home, little requests were surreptitiously put in for reaction, such as placing an order for Starbucks coffee instead of regular brands. Once supplied with same, they knew that someone was paying attention to them and their activities.

Also working in the country at the time were elements of the elite Green Berets special forces, who acted as mentors for the Northern Alliance, providing equipment, training and heavy firepower, courtesy of AC-130 Spectre gunships, B-52 bombers and precision strike aircraft. They quickly learned not to tell the Afghan men about how to fight, as they all deemed themselves natural warriors. To imply anything else was a gross insult to them. Instead, they learned gently to encourage them to fight in a different way than was previously practised. However, old habits die hard.

Other cultural differences also caused some interesting situations. In Afghan male culture, women are deemed second-class citizens and, in their eyes, only serve two purposes: child bearing and home making. As for other men, that's a different story, as they are there for fun, fighting and entertainment; and the sight of young, athletic western men amongst them was interesting. Apparently, the more experienced soldiers quickly learned to talk up their personal and everlasting commitments to their partners back home, so as not to hurt the feelings of anyone making advances, while the young, single and dumb avoided rampant Afghan warriors like the plague. Tom Carew of the SAS, who trained the Mujahideen in their fight against the Soviets, referred to the same phenomenon somewhat obliquely in an interview given to the *Sunday Telegraph* in 2001: 'Another priority [in training] was banning the slings that they used to strap their weapons to their backs. They pinned religious tokens on them, which jingled as they trudged up the narrow mountain paths or waist deep in snow. I explained that there is only one place for a guerrilla's gun: in his hands. Poised. Ready for use. They realized the logic quickly, but I have to confess to an ulterior

US Special Forces with the Northern Alliance.

motive, too. Among the Mujahideen, it is common practice to walk along holding hands. It sounds astonishing. It is a cultural thing, but a habit I didn't intend to indulge.'

The other major contributor of special forces to Afghanistan after 9/11 was the UK, providing both SAS and SBS units on the scene very quickly. By sheer coincidence, they had been training near Afghanistan prior to 9/11, which enabled a rapid response once their services were requested by the US government. People often forget that 9/11 was a major terrorist incident for the UK also, despite more than 30 years of terrorism emanating from the 'Troubles' in Northern Ireland. A lot of innocent British people were killed and injured on 9/11 in the Twin Towers. In some ways, Britain was in a much better position to respond to the events of 9/11 than America was. This was due to the fact that the UK had massive land, air and sea assets already deployed in the Gulf of Oman as part of Exercise Saif Sareea II (Swift Sword), and these were quickly put at the disposal of the United States. Swift Sword involved forces from the UK and Oman, and was full-on, with over 22,000 personnel, 6,500 vehicles, more than 20 naval vessels and 40 helicopters, plus about 50 fixed-wing aircraft. (You may dimly remember the complaints about Challenger 2 tanks dying in the desert because of inadequate filter systems.)

As generous as this offer was, America only required two specific items from the UK: special forces and tanker aircraft. The British SAS were of course no strangers to Afghanistan, as they had gained considerable experience working in the country through their support for the Mujahideen against the Russians. The tempo of operations quickly increased, with the SAS providing targeting data, reconnaissance and surveillance capability, as well as direct support for Northern Alliance operations against the Taliban.

With the unconventional war well under way, George W. Bush issued an ultimatum to the Taliban: either turn Osama bin Laden and his Al-Qaeda supporters in, or face the consequences. As the days ticked by, it was crystal clear that the Taliban had no intention of complying with America's request and on the contrary, threatened them with an all-out Jihad (holy war). Although there was no set deadline for the commencement of military action, the tactical planners were ever mindful of the onset of winter and the closing window of opportunity for precision air strikes. Beyond this, and they would be facing a rerun of events in Kosovo and clearly nobody wanted that. As the tension mounted, reports started to circulate that both UK and US special forces had been involved in serious skirmishes in Northern Afghanistan; all of course denied by the powers that be. On October 7, the phoney war ended, when multiple air attacks commenced against Taliban air-defence systems, fortifications and command and control centres. Although much of the intelligence for these air strikes was garnered from satellites and air reconnaissance assets, some had clearly been provided by covert,

British SBS in Afghanistan.

ground-based units operating from a US base in Uzbekistan, and as a result accuracy was extremely high; unlike Iraq, where command and control nodes were sited deep underground and hard to get at. The Taliban's were completely the opposite. Generally, their command centres were little more than mud walled compounds that stood little chance against precision guided munitions. But worse was yet to come for them. Up until 9/11, they had a pretty level playing field against the forces of the Northern Alliance, almost fighting with a WWI-style mentality. This folly was accomplished by means of trench systems that ran across the ridges overlooking the valleys and strategic road junctions: great for defence against a rag-tag army, but hopeless against special forces directing precision air attacks.

The difference special forces made in Afghanistan cannot be underestimated, as a major force multiplier for the Northern Alliance (see p. 36). At the start of military operations in September 2001, the Northern Alliance's fielded forces were based primarily in north-western Afghanistan, and numbered some 15,000 men, while their sworn enemy, the Taliban, dominated the eastern part of the country and fielded around 50,000 soldiers, together with several hundred Al-Qaeda terrorists. Although enthusiastic and well motivated, prior to the involvement of western special forces, the Northern Alliance had regained very little territory from the Taliban since being ousted by them. Within weeks of special forces support, they made substantial territory gains, and at the same time greatly increased the numbers in their ranks. Although proud of their own military achievements, they delighted in watching the Taliban being annihilated by the B-52s that roamed the skies far above them. Often this was done by means of carpet bombing, but occasionally it took the form of air burst munitions – which quite literally sucked the Taliban fighters out of their trenches and vaporized them in mid-air. A sight that frightened all who witnessed it, including the fighters of the Northern Alliance.

Although de facto allies of the West, by virtue of their being a proxy force, the Northern Alliance were not without their problems. On one particular work-up phase, prior to an attack on a Taliban stronghold, an SAS team was instructing Northern Alliance soldiers in the art of assaulting an enemy position while under fire and were so impressed with their progress that they brought the attack time forward. This was, however, a decision they would later regret. As the Northern Alliance soldiers reached their objective, they suddenly and without warning abandoned the British Army tactics, techniques and procedure they had been taught. In a scene that would not have been out of place in a Rambo movie, or maybe *Lawrence of Arabia*, they attacked by means of horsemen, who carried out in effect an 18th-century cavalry charge. But the madness didn't end there. The rest of the force, who were supposedly providing covering fire, decided to sit down and watch the spectacle without firing a shot. Fortunately for them all, the Taliban fled.

Similar situations also confronted the US Green Berets. One example was a fierce firefight for a bridge that dominated a gorge. With both the Taliban and the Northern Alliance merrily blazing away at one another, they all suddenly noticed a car speeding towards the bridge. Without any orders or warnings, they both stopped firing and let the car drive over the bridge without hindrance. Once it was safely out of the way, they commenced firing again, much to the bemusement of the US special forces. One Green Beret then enquired as to the reason for the safe passage for the car and was told that the driver was the local taxi man, and that he plied his services for both sides. So he clearly couldn't be shot at! Radio procedure wasn't always out of the manual either. Often during firefights each side would taunt the other over their radios as to how bad their opponents shooting was. Bizarrely, they would often make comments like 'You missed me by 10 metres that time' or 'That one was a near one.' Needless to say, the more

Northern Alliance soldiers take cover behind a dead Taliban fighter.

Northern Alliance fighting the Taliban at Qali-e-Jhangi.

savvy British and Americans quickly used this information to bracket mortar rounds right upon the Taliban's positions.

SPECIAL FORCES

There is no doubt in my mind that the use of special forces in Afghanistan, prior to the commencement of official, conventional action, was both decisive and critical to the initial success against the Taliban and Al-Qaeda forces operating in-country. It is fair to say that the Taliban never knew what hit them in the months that followed 9/11, as their military prowess simply wasn't up to the mark when it came to fighting modern, well equipped forces. By 2002, they were on the ropes. For the special forces involved in Afghanistan during this period, life was extremely busy! In addition to fighting Al-Qaeda and the Taliban, they also carried out numerous 'hearts and minds' missions. One particularly effective effort was marking out safe lanes for the dropping of humanitarian food ration packs from the air to the starving Afghan people, as the use of vehicles at this time was just too dangerous and impractical.There was also the issue of mines; Afghanistan still has millions of them littering the landscape and the marking out of safe zones saved many innocent lives. This particular operation was of immense importance, as the United States had promised the Afghan people food and shelter and by delivering it, they had made friends, rather than enemies.

With this operation over, special forces began engaging in direct attacks on Al-Qaeda and Taliban training camps located throughout Afghanistan, especially around the lower slopes of the southern Hindu Kush mountains and near Bagram airfield. The training camps were generally well hidden, and often featured cave complexes that were virtually impossible to detect from the air. This often meant tasking an SAS team with a CTR (Close Target Reconnaissance) – always a dangerous mission, as you will always be outnumbered if compromised.

British SAS in Landrover. Soon after this photo was taken a US Chinook landed on top of an SAS Landrover at Qali-e-Jhangi causing serious injuries to one of the special forces soldiers, known only as Soldier J. He received £1 million in compensation from the UK MoD. A further eighty such cases from Iraq and Afghanistan are apparently being considered.

A British SAS trooper rushes to the aid of a wounded colleague who has just sustained a head wound.

In comparing the British and American special forces, it must be said that both operated extremely well, but with the SAS having the slight tactical edge initially, as they could draw on previous operational experience gained in Aden and Oman. This was to be of great importance during the first few months of deployment in Afghanistan. The US special forces teams had little comparable combat experience in such an environment and therefore sought the advice of the SAS. This was provided by means of small four-man teams who were assigned to them as advisors. It was a routine quid pro quo arrangement, as the US often provided AC-130 Spectre gunships and Little Bird light attack helicopters in support of British operations. Each had something to offer the other. This was just as well, as during one incident in 2002, the smooth running wheels of the coalition wagon almost came off and only the outstanding combat skills of a few saved it.

TALIBAN REVOLT AT QALI-E-JHANGI

The incident occurred after a major battle for the strategically important Bagram airfield, located near Mazar-e-Sharif. To this day, there is still a dispute over exactly what happened and who was to blame. It all started when a major offensive to clear the Taliban from the areas immediately around the Bagram airfield – by means of the Northern Alliance – went so well that the Taliban forces were utterly routed and surrendered in their hundreds. This was good news for the American CIA operatives, as they could garner fresh intelligence on Al-Qaeda and assess how effective the campaign raging against them was going. Usually, after a battle, the prisoners were split into two categories: Afghans and foreign fighters. For the Afghans taken prisoner, good treatment was generally their lot and more often than not, they were released after giving an undertaking that they would never bear arms against their Afghan brothers again. Some would even throw the towel in completely, and denounce the Taliban – and enlist in the

The imposing Qali-e-Jhangi fortress. Its name means 'House of War' – a very apt title.

Northern Alliance's cause instead. However, for the foreign fighters – mainly Pakistani – life wasn't so good, as they were often mistreated and on some occasions even executed in cold blood by Northern Alliance forces in front of their American sponsors. The Americans were understandably extremely sensitive to these acts, and where possible tried to take the Taliban prisoners from them to ensure their protection. But this was not always possible. The Americans feared a repeat of a previous atrocity, when Northern Alliance fighters had machine-gunned an entire vehicle convoy of metal containers containing Taliban prisoners, later claiming that they had only been creating ventilation holes. The decision was taken to move the Bagram prisoners to the impressive mud-walled fortress of Qali-e-Jhangi, located near Mazar-e-Sharif.

In theory, this decision was right and proper, as it protected the prisoners' welfare and human rights. But inside the

US Special Forces during the Taliban revolt at Qali-e-Jhangi.

Northern Alliance soldier gunned down at Qali-e-Jhangi. Sadly, despite American medical aid, he later died of his head wound.

compound, all was not well amongst the Taliban prisoners. A feeling of increasing restlessness and apprehension had manifested itself within their ranks and clearly, revolt was in the air. The spark soon came, when during a prisoner interrogation, CIA SOG operative Johnny (Mike) Spann was brutally murdered, along with his Northern Alliance bodyguards, causing all hell to break loose. Within minutes, fierce firefights were raging across the compound between the Taliban prisoners and the Northern Alliance, leaving the vulnerable Americans in a desperate position. US special forces on hand called in air strikes directly on the compound, but this still wasn't enough to quell things. By this time hundreds lay dead, and still the battle raged for the fortress. Fearing a catastrophe, US special forces called in the support of nearby British special forces, both SAS and SBS.They arrived in spectacular style, in a small fleet of dirty white land Rovers, bristling with machine guns. Wasting no time, the soldiers quickly put on masks to disguise their identities, which naturally made them look sinister and threatening, as did their clothing, a mixture of both Afghan and military styles.

When it came to the fighting, there was no doubt about who these men were. Forming a six-man skirmish line, they charged the Taliban positions within the fort with all their machine-guns blazing away, raining lead on anyone who dared show their presence. The effect was devastating. Spurred on by the British special forces action, the US and Northern Alliance soldiers took the initiative and regained control of the compound. Inside, it was a bloody scene from hell, with bodies strewn everywhere. The outside world was outraged and the reverberations from that day are still felt. The British special forces nevertheless were the heroes of the hour for the military establishment and several were invited to Washington DC to be presented with America's highest award, the Congressional Medal of Honor. Speaking of the British special forces at the time, Defense Secretary Donald

Rumsfeld commented: 'They are among the best soldiers in the world, and are truly exceptional men.'

LOOKING FOR ELVIS

After the Qali-e-Jhangi revolt, the Taliban began falling back towards their safe havens, such as Kandahar, as there was little sanctuary for them elsewhere. It seemed like every time they made a stand anywhere, they lost. Around this time, America's priority shifted from the destruction of the Taliban to the apprehension or killing of Al-Qaeda's front man, Osama bin Laden. Although understandable at the time, this change of focus let the Taliban off the hook, and gave a sizable part of their force a chance to rearm and retrain in Helmand province in Southern Afghanistan. Today, we are paying for that fateful decision. For America, Osama bin Laden was a thorn in their side and they wanted him gone. They had of course tried targeting him during President Clinton's tenure, by means of cruise missiles; but had failed abysmally. His propaganda videos showed he was still alive and well, and clearly a threat, despite the massive bombing campaign and intense special forces search operations. At this time, Osama bin Laden seemed to be appearing everywhere, coining the term, 'Elvis Sightings'. On one operation, intel had reported a sighting of him in an Al-Qaeda/Taliban training camp near Kandahar, in southern Afghanistan. Although this was not fully verified and authenticated, the decision was taken to launch a ground attack by the British SAS. This decision was prompted by the then growing realization that bombing missions alone did not always achieve the right results; for one thing the aggressors could never be sure that they had got everybody they wanted. (To take one example of how things could go wrong, American aircraft bombed some cave complexes, trapping some Taliban fighters inside. They then summoned more aircraft to finish the job but the second bombing mission cleared away the rock debris that was blocking the cave's entrance, thereby releasing the trapped Taliban.)

For the SAS, this was to be their biggest raid since being deployed in 2001 and even by their standards, it was an intensely demanding mission. The defenders of this training camp had sworn to fight to the death and previous experience suggested that they were not bluffing. So as to achieve maximum speed, aggression and surprise, the SAS attacked with two squadrons comprising some 100 highly trained and well-armed soldiers. All were experienced in this type of warfare. As they fought there way towards the centre of the camp, they came under intense fire from all directions. Some of the defensive positions had already been identified prior to the attack and these were quickly neutralized. But others came into play that could not have been anticipated, as they were well hidden in the sides of a ridge that ran along a deep, steep-sided gully. These locations hid both machine guns and RPGs and rained heavy fire onto the advancing SAS soldiers. Realizing that they were in a precarious position, the SAS divided their teams so as to both draw and suppress incoming fire. This tactic was just beginning to work, when a large force of Taliban and Al-Qaeda fighters suddenly appeared from an underground bunker via a hidden cave entrance and tried to outflank them. These fighters meant business and were hell-bent on the destruction of the SAS force that had dared to enter their backyard.

With the now serious threat of being overrun, the SAS decided simply to advance in a rapid, classic charge, aiming at one point for maximum effect. This brought them face-to-face with the defenders, and hand-to-hand combat ensued. Nearby, a small HQ element of the SAS who had been relaying communications back to the main base saw that their fellow troopers were fighting for their lives, and raced to their aid. Their action caught the Taliban and Al-Qaeda fighters off guard, and broke their counter-attack, forcing them to flee back along the gully. After several long minutes of intense fighting, the action was won, leaving 27 enemy dead and 35 wounded, all at the cost of four wounded. Decorations were later bestowed on some of the SAS men for their actions, but for obvious security reasons, I cannot reveal the names of those heroes who fought so bravely that day.

TORA BORA

Around late November 2001, reports also began filtering through that Osama bin Laden had been tracked down to the Tora Bora cave complexes just south of Jalalabad, near the border with Pakistan. This immediately resulted in a major operation being mounted. At first, it was just a case of precision bombing, followed up by carefully targeted special forces operations. But this was found to be totally inadequate to cope with the numbers of Al-Qaeda and Taliban operating within the caves. More ground follow-up strategies were required, such as sweep and clear missions and highly dangerous cave clearing operations. These were generally performed by British, American and Australian special forces in conjunction with the Northern Alliance – as it was extremely important for them to be seen participating in such operations. Such activities, it was hoped, would create stability and confidence in the various factions and tribes that made up the Northern Alliance, as they one day would be key critical to the long-term security of Afghanistan and its elected government. This was to prove a wise and prudent policy, as northern Afghanistan is now a relatively peaceful place, compared to the utter bedlam that exists in the southern provinces.

OPERATION ANACONDA

Despite the best efforts of all concerned in the Tora Bora campaign, no trace of Osama bin Laden was found. He had escaped, yet again (if he had ever been there). Feeling frustrated, the special forces teams redoubled their efforts. Their diligent and painstaking work eventually paid off when a small British SBS team identified a fortified Al-Qaeda position that seemed unduly well protected and equipped, compared with others that they had observed. After intense surveillance, the SBS recce team confirmed that Osama bin Laden was indeed there, along with other high-value targets, Ayman Al-Zawahiri and Mullah Omar – the leaders of Al-Qaeda and the Taliban – and communicated that a ground assault force should be sent in immediately. The SBS even identified and mapped out helicopter insertion LZ's in the adjacent valley for the incoming force, as this would give them the safest and most covert route in. Fearing the worst, that he might escape again, the British deployed cut-off groups at each end of the valley that the fortification was in. They urgently requested more support, but were denied it, as the UK did not have enough military assets in the region to go it alone. There was also a political reason: 9/11 was America's tragedy, so it seemed more appropriate to give US forces the kudos for finding and destroying bin Laden.

Although bitterly disappointed, the SBS reluctantly accepted this order and withdrew to the adjacent valley to await the arrival of the Americans. But none came. They waited another day, but still no Americans. Finally, on 2 March 2002, three days later, they arrived in force – but in the wrong valley. Instead of landing in the adjacent valley as previously advised and sneaking up on the target, they landed slap bang in the middle of the target valley: and walked into the jaws of hell, as they would later state.

For the Americans, this was their biggest operation since Tora Bora, and they code-named it Anaconda. Operation Anaconda's aim was to conduct a large-scale, combined operation with the Afghan military forces in the Shahi-Kot valley and Arma mountains, southeast of Zormat, and destroy all Al-Qaeda and Taliban forces found there. Operation

Anaconda comprised elements of the 10th Mountain Division, 101st Airborne Division, the US special forces groups, TF 11, TF Bowie and TF Dagger; plus British Royal Marines (SBS), Canada's 3rd Battalion, Princess Patricia's Canadian Light Infantry, the Afghan National Army, the German KSK, and elements of the Australian and New Zealand SASR, who acted as cut-off and blocking groups in the adjacent valleys. In its sheer size, the force was impressive, consisting of some 1,700 US personnel, 1,000 Afghan militia and several hundred other coalition soldiers. The initial estimation of enemy forces situated in the Shahi-Kot valley prior to Operation Anaconda was said to be in the region of 200-plus. However, as the operation commenced, and enemy reinforcements poured in from neighbouring valleys, the figure rose to around 1,000 fighters.

Why US Commanders ignored British advice at the time of Operation Anaconda is still a subject of much heated debate, especially so amongst the US forces involved in it. It seems that America still hadn't learned the value of good intelligence. During the operation itself, US forces were plagued with problems from start to finish and only through sheer dogged determination did they prevail. On occasions, helicopters ferrying in troops got shot to pieces inserting them in one place, only to find out that the LZ was wrong, which necessitated a return trip under even more intense fire. The British had warned the Americans that the target valley walls and ridges were bristling with machine gun, mortar and RPG nests that had excellent arcs of fire. Every single spot that could take a helicopter had been pre-targeted in the mortar pits, so landing in the valley was lethal.

One of the key fighting platforms that saved US and coalition forces on the ground from certain disaster was the Apache attack helicopter. The pilots flying these machines performed miracles, often flying straight at the Taliban positions to draw fire away from their buddies on the ground. Operation

Australian SASR blocking team during Operation Anaconda.

Anaconda's commander, Major General Franklin L. 'Buster' Hagenback had the best intentions in the world when he drew up his OPLAN: but friction, as Karl von Clauswitz would have put it, was against him. Big time.

Hagenback's plan was to use overwhelming and superior force to seal the Shahi-Kot valley and all its rat runs and then strike, hard and fast. TF Hammer, the assault force, comprised Afghan militia and US special forces, TF Anvil, the blocking role, was assigned to the 3rd Brigade ('Rakkasans') of the 101st Airborne Division, led by Colonel Frank Wiercinski, and 1st Battalion, 87th Regiment (1-87) of the 10th Mountain Division, led by Lieutenant Colonel Paul La Camera. For fire support, Hagenback had USAF aircraft, rather than artillery; the latter would surely have been more effective.

From the get-go things went wrong. It all started around midnight on March 2, 2002, as units of TF Hammer were heading out towards the target valley, after leaving their base in Gardez. A convoy consisting of Afghan militia led by Zia Lodin and accompanied by Special Forces A-Team Texas began to lose

US Chinook inserting troops at the height of Operation Anaconda. If only they had read up on the Soviet experience in the same valley – when the entire force was annihilated – this bitter action could have been avoided.

vehicles in a series of accidents as they travelled along a poorly defined route. Fearing more losses, they ordered the turning on of headlights, which gave away their position and alerted the Taliban to their intended route. As if that wasn't bad enough, an element of the Third Special Forces Group who were in the convoy decided to break off, and head for their assigned RV point directly, as they were concerned about falling behind schedule. Tragically, as a result of their detour, high above them an AC-130 Spectre gunship (Grim 31), which was riding shotgun for the Task Force, mistook them for an enemy convoy and proceeded to strafe them, killing the American Officer leading the force, and wounding several of his men. Finally, the convoy reached its objective, only to find that the 55-minute bombardment that they had been promised had now been cut back to just six bombs – meaning that they were going to be hit by everything that the Taliban had waiting for them.

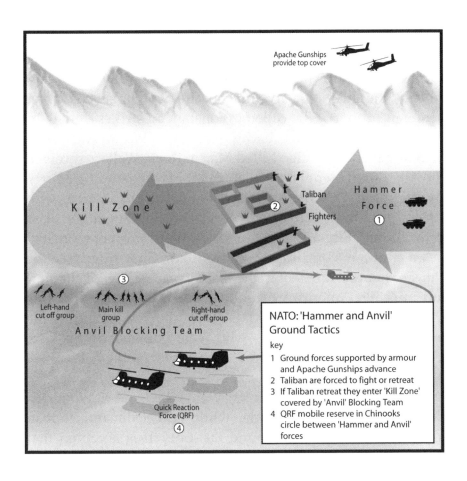

Apache Gunships provide top cover

Kill Zone

Taliban

Fighters

Hammer Force

①

②

③

Left-hand cut off group

Main kill group

Right-hand cut off group

Anvil Blocking Team

Quick Reaction Force (QRF)

④

NATO: 'Hammer and Anvil' Ground Tactics

key

1 Ground forces supported by armour and Apache Gunships advance
2 Taliban are forced to fight or retreat
3 If Taliban retreat they enter 'Kill Zone' covered by 'Anvil' Blocking Team
4 QRF mobile reserve in Chinooks circle between 'Hammer and Anvil' forces

Meanwhile, the TF Anvil element had their own problems to contend with. As they landed their first chalks on the eastern and northern edges of the valley, they were hit with heavy enemy fire from all along the ridge line. They had been led to believe that all of the 150 enemy forces that were their targets were located in a village at the base of the valley. But instead, they encountered some 500 hardened fighters in their LZ. They fought all day long, until being extracted by helicopter further down the valley. This extraction was only made possible by the sheer tenacity and courage of other special forces acting in support, who called in constant air strikes from B-2s, B-52s, F-15s and F-16s orbiting overhead. One, an Australian SAS Regiment signaller, called Martin 'Jock' Wallace received the Australian Medal for Gallantry for his outstanding efforts. By this time, 28 Americans lay wounded in the area, with several hundred Taliban and Al-Qaeda fighters either dead or wounded. Elsewhere in the valley, there was yet more bad news after a major disaster on the Takur Ghar ridge (see the full story of this incident in the *Chariots of the Damned* chapter) left multiple American casualties, and saw the loss of two Chinook helicopters. Other incidents followed, including the awful death of 14 civilians who were bombed by mistake, leaving some to wonder about the need for, and effectiveness of, such an operation.

In all, eight American soldiers were killed and 72 wounded during Operation Anaconda, while Al-Qaeda and Taliban losses are estimated at around 800-plus. It is accepted that a lot of Taliban fighters slipped through the net, and ended up in either Pakistan or southern Afghanistan. On March 18, 2002 General Tommy Franks declared Operation Anaconda officially over, describing it as 'an unqualified and complete success'. For many others however, the jury was still out. Some dispute the estimated Taliban losses. There was also bad feeling between the British and Americans over the Royal Marines post-Operation Anaconda mopping-up operation,

Air strikes during Operation Anaconda.

because they never came across a single Al-Qaeda or Taliban fighter. This prompted the American Army magazine *Stars and Stripes* to describe their performance as disappointing. The Royal Marines however, took (and take) the view that had the Americans not wasted three days, Osama bin Laden and his cohorts would have been either killed or captured in the initial phase of the operation.

The Canadians had one remarkable result during the operation. One of their snipers, Corporal Rob Furlong of the Princess Patricia's Canadian Light Infantry, broke a 25-year record for the world's longest combat kill by a sniper. Using a MacMillan long-range TAC-50 .50-calibre sniper rifle, he picked off a Taliban fighter armed with an RPK machine gun at a confirmed distance of 2,430 metres (1.51 miles); an outstanding achievement.

For American citizens mourning the tragedy of 9/11, the coalition soldiers fighting for and on behalf of them were their 'Avenging Angels'. Had the military planners and strategists not taken their eye off Afghanistan and focused on Iraq instead, perhaps we would not still be engaging in intense combat operations in Helmand Province.

Princess Patricia's Canadian Light Infantry snipers MCpl Tim McMeekin, MCpl Graham Ragsdale, MCpl Arron Perry, Cpl Dennis Eason and Cpl Rob Furlong were awared the Bronze Star by the US for their actions during Operation Anaconda.

Canadian sniper in action.

Soldiers of the US 101st Airborne take a breather during Operation Anaconda.

Operation Anaconda: A US soldier with a .50 cal HMG looks out for Taliban activity in the valley.

US Forces clear a house during Operation Viper.

A soldier from the US 101st Airborne ducks his head to avoid incoming fire.

US Forces take a Taliban suspect into custody.

US Forces in action at Spin Baldak.

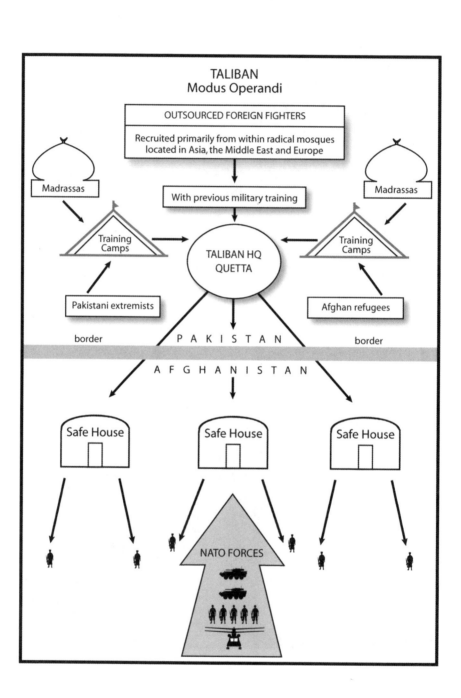

III

The Taliban

Since 9/11, the word 'Taliban' has come into increasingly common usage in our everyday language as we discuss the situation in Afghanistan. And yet, precious few people actually know much about them. For most, they are simply nothing more than bearded men with turbans who go around shooting at our troops every chance they get and will soon get their comeuppance. But, for the few that fight them, they are known to be tenacious, articulate and courageous fighters who, despite serious losses and defeats, just keep coming back. What we are fighting is not so much a force of soldiers as such, but a medieval ideology that is gaining more and more popularity in the modern Muslim world – especially in Pakistan. The Taliban are, in essence, a Sunni Islamist and Pashtun nationalist movement that has tasted power in Afghanistan once already, from 1996 through to their fall in 2001. Like all tyrannical regimes, it wants to rule again. The word Taliban, is the Pashto plural form of the Arabic word Talib, which means student. This is very apt, as the members of this group are generally drawn from students of religious seminaries and madrassas, located mainly in Pakistan and Afghanistan. Whilst they were in power in Afghanistan, the world at large showed little interest in the Taliban and their aspirations. As a result, they had a free hand. That was of course, until 9/11; then the West was extremely interested in the Taliban and their ideology. Prior to that, the only states and countries that diplomatically recognized the Taliban were the United Arab Emirates, Pakistan and Saudi Arabia.

A Talib fighter beating women. Photograph by a courageous member of the RAWA (Revolutionary Association of the Women of Afghanistan), who struggle for human rights, democracy and secularism in Afghanistan.

BIRTH OF THE TALIBAN

The Taliban were created in 1993, by Naseerullah Baber, an interior minister during Benazir Bhutto's second Pakistan government from 1993–1996, in conjunction with the Pakistani military and their ISI secret service.This was done in the province of Quetta – now the epicentre for terrorism and extremism in Pakistan – the general idea being to form a militia, consisting of religious students recruited from madrassas within Pakistan. Their mission was to gain control of the Afghan Mujahideen government. Their first reported foray into Afghanistan was in 1994, when 30 of their number freed two girls who had been kidnapped and raped by local Afghan commanders. This story quickly circulated around Afghanistan, attracting more recruits with a desire to adopt their spiritually rigorous and self-abnegating ideals. Soon after, some 200 Taliban seized the trading town of Spin Baldak, thus furnishing themselves with an instant supply route from Pakistan. A further bonus was the liberation of an arms dump containing some 18,000 Kalashnikov assault rifles, artillery pieces, ammunition and vehicles. So as to gain credibility, the Taliban started to provide protection for trade delegations and outside visitors, as travel around Afghanistan then was very risky (though when has it ever been Pullman class?). This became quite a lucrative operation and in time led them to seize and control several major towns and cities, including Kandahar.

Alarmed at their rapid rise, the Rabbani government of the day refused to recognize or accept the Pakistani-sponsored Taliban, and thus a protracted conflict developed. The struggle was mainly focussed around south Kabul, Herat and Kunduz. As Pakistan's creation grew in power in Afghanistan, more money and aid poured in from Saudi Arabia to help with their rapid expansion. It was at this time that the Taliban started to adopt their now infamous strictures on piety, austerity, and the obligations and roles of men in their society. This is believed to have been derived from the Deobandi school of thought, originally from India. With an ever increasing army of followers, the Taliban needed a front man; the movement prior to this had been largely faceless. Up stepped Mullah Mohammed Omar. Pakistan of course supported him initially, as they felt that they had him in their pocket. This proved to be a bad decision, and one that they would bitterly regret. Mullah Omar was at this time riding so high in the popularity stakes that he could call the shots. That would have been fine, if he was singing from the same hymn sheet (or maybe a less inappropriate metaphor, interpreting the Koran in the same way) as the Pakistani government; but he wasn't. Like any leader, he wanted to leave his stamp of authority and direction on the movement, but it was his method of doing this, rather than his motivation, that was wrong. For him, more radical fundamentalists equals more recruits – which was true to a point. But then, there are fundamentalists, and there are extremists, and his choices seemed to be the latter. Having such eschatologically committed people meant that the movement began to get more extreme in its ideology, leaving Pakistan less and less in control of its direction.

UNCLE SAM AND THE TALIBAN

Pakistan at this time, of course did not want to admit to losing its grip on the Taliban and therefore set about devising a strategy that would rein them in – but at the same time, give them more influence in the region.Their ploy was to seduce the Americans into believing that the Taliban could rid Afghanistan of all Jihadi groups and restore the old monarch, Zahir Shah, to power. It all sounded very plausible, and the US bought into it. To be fair to Pakistan, there were members of the Taliban, such as Mohammad Rabbani (not related to Burhanuddin Rabbani of the Northern Alliance) who genuinely did want Zahir Shah back, as did others. But they were in the minority. America, believing the hype, threw money, weapons and intelligence the Taliban's way. With their help, and indeed that of the UK also, the Taliban gained control of almost 80% of the country within two years. But unsurprisingly in retrospect, they reneged on the promise of giving back power and control to Zahir Shah. The Taliban had arrived.

TALIBAN VERSUS THE NORTHERN ALLIANCE

In the mid 1990s, the only factions that threatened the Taliban were those that made up the Northern Alliance. But even there, allegiances were flexible. General Abdul Malik (General Abdul Rashid Dostom's third in command) would temporarily side with the Taliban at Mazar-e-Sharif and overthrow Dostom – only to betray the Taliban soon after and switch sides again. This reversal of loyalties was prompted by his certainty that they were about to be massacred in their thousands; an orgy of violence that he participated in. The Taliban later came back to Mazar-e-Sharif and returned the compliment, by murdering thousands in their turn.

The only individual at that time who even remotely stood a chance of defeating the Taliban was Ahmad Shah Massoud. Although he engaged them in combat on many occasions, he never totally defeated them. The nearest he came to total victory was on the Shamali plains, where he organized carefully set up ambushes in conjunction with local people. Once again, after the intial setback, the Taliban returned and massacred all the young fighting men in that region, after having expelled most of the local population from the region.

OSAMA BIN LADEN AND THE TALIBAN

Around the same time as the Taliban and Northern Alliance were battling it out, Osama bin Laden arrived in Afghanistan from Sudan, and quickly sided with the Taliban.This was signified by an alliance of the Taliban and bin Laden's Al-Qaeda-trained 055 Brigade. The partnership only lasted from 1997 to 2001, as by then Osama bin Laden had much greater plans for his organization. Part of the strength of the relationship between the two organizations was drawn from the marriage of one of bin Laden's sons to Mullah Omar's daughter. A stronger binding force was finance. Osama bin Laden was underwriting the activites of the Taliban via Saudi Arabia. This close and intense relationship helps explain why the Taliban risked so much in protecting him from the wrath of the United States, both after the 1998 US embassy bombings in Tanzania and Kenya, and following 9/11. Although indicted in US criminal courts for these actions, through satellite phone records and sworn testimony, the Taliban would not give him up or indicate where he was hiding out.

Even after 9/11, they continued to harbour him – protesting his innocence to all that would listen – while at the same time offering to hand him over to a neutral third party, unallied to the United States. Finally, America's patience ran out, and the following five point ultimatum was issued to the Taliban:

1. Deliver to the US all of the leaders of Al-Qaeda.
2. Release all imprisoned foreign nationals.
3. Close immediately every terrorist training camp.
4. Hand over every terrorist and their supporters to appropriate authorities.
5. Give the United States full access to terrorist training camps for inspection.

Needless to say, the Taliban rejected this ultimatum on September 21, 2001, stating that there was no evidence linking Osama bin Laden to the attacks of September 11. Very soon after, America gave its response. In 2004 bin Laden admitted to ordering the attacks on New York and Washington, in a videotape broadcast on Al Jazeera. No doubt, there were some in the Taliban who were none too happy about this broadcast, as they had suffered greatly for siding with Mr bin Laden.

At the time of writing, the leader of the Taliban movement is still Mullah Mohammed Omar, who continues to surround himself with lieutenants made up in the main of village mullahs and senior members of the Islamic religious schools in Pakistan.

RECRUITING FOR THE CAUSE

Despite the intense operations of NATO, recruiting still continues unabated, with an estimated 96% of the Taliban's current strength still derived from the Pashtuns of Afghanistan and Northern Pakistan. However, in recent years, some of its latest recruits have hailed from Europe and even China. The UK has the highest number of Muslim extremists and potential terrorists in Europe, earning (via the capital) the nickname of Londistan. The term is in common use amongst western intelligence agencies. For the Taliban, this is excellent news, as they can exploit Britain's vulnerable Muslim youth very easily. This is usually done within radical mosques in the UK. The cauldron of anti-western sentiment is stirred, to see who bites. Anyone who does is invited over to one of the many Pakistani madrassas that specialise in preaching hatred and loathing for the infidel, although officially, the 'students' are there for supposedly more religious study. And then it's a Taliban training camp in Pakistan. Thereafter, you're in Helmand Province, fighting, in some cases, your own British countrymen. Those who really shine get to go back to the UK, as either recruiters or sleepers; and so the cycle starts again.

In this dramatic image captured at Qali-e-Jhangi, a Talib fighter (top left) can be seen opening fire on Northern Alliance soldiers who are dropping grenades into a Taliban fox hole in the centre of the fortress.

Canadian soldiers assist locals in digging their car out of the snow.

The New York-based Human Rights Watch estimates that the Taliban killed seven hundred civilians in 2006. Human Rights Watch contends that attacks on civilians by the Taliban and other insurgents were war crimes, because 'they intentionally targeted civilian objects that served no military purpose, including schools, buses or bazaars.'

IV

The Devil's Harvest

Aside from the Taliban, America and its NATO allies have another major issue to deal with in Afghanistan: the opium poppy, the plant used to make heroin and morphine. For the people of Afghanistan, this is their number-one export – and taking it away from them will be no easy task. Almost 3,000,000 people in Afghanistan derive their income from its cultivation, directly and indirectly. That equates to 12% of the country's population. It is of course the most profitable product that Afghanistan produces – and in a country that has precious little else in the way of natural resources. We have one hell of a problem to deal with. Afghanistan now produces up to 90% of the world's opium poppy supply, with around 45% of it going to the West, some 3% for internal Afghan use – and a whopping 52% for its neighbour, Iran. Its end-supplier profitability is staggering. A farmer will sell a bag of resin to a dealer for around $35 US. The dealer will then export it in 800-kilo batches, as this is apparently the preferred shipping quantity. This will then end up in our American and European cities with a street price of some $6,000,000 US. With this sort of money to be made it is no surprise to hear that our troops are struggling to wean the Afghanis off its cultivation. To an average Afghan farmer, it is 10 times more profitable to them than growing wheat. But as Afghanistan's President Hamid Karzai warned: 'If we don't destroy the opium trade, then it will destroy us.'

Opium poppy growth is not a new phenomenon to Afghanistan, it has been around for centuries. The only group of people who ever came close to stamping it out were the Taliban. Their first efforts in banning the growth of the poppy were in 1997 but were totally ineffectual as they did not bother to enforce the new proscription. This was a deliberate oversight, as they realised that there was a fortune to be had from the drugs racket, religious beliefs notwithstanding. And they were now the main traffickers. In 2000, Afghanistan's opium production accounted for some 75% of the world's supply. But this figure fell dramatically in the following months, after the Taliban issued another decree banning its cultivation. This time, it was enforced vigorously and anyone found to be either growing poppy or trafficking its fruits faced serious consequences, not short of execution. As a result, between July 27, 2000 and February 2001 production fell by 98%. However, this dip didn't last for long: as once the Taliban regime collapsed, the Northern Alliance took up production from where they had left off. Production rose again dramatically in their areas, to a then record of 87% of the world's opium supply. This was confirmed in 2005, during a detailed analysis of the crisis that Afghanistan was facing.

To stem the tide, the British government suggested paying the farmers compensation in return for them not growing poppy. In theory, it sounded a good idea, but it backfired spectacularly when all the other farmers who were *not* cultivating opium decided to jump on the bandwagon. They stopped growing conventional crops and began growing opium poppy instead, to share in the bonanza. Needless to say, production soared again, to a record high. According to the UN, in 2006 the area of Afghanistan now under opium poppy cultivation is 78% greater than in 2005. The figure was ascertained by means of satellite imagery and ground surveys, which showed 185,000 hectares of poppy fields, compared to 104,000 the previous year.

The yield of opium is determined by various factors such as weather and water availability and this in turn affects the price paid for it. A good crop would be deemed around 39kg of poppy per hectare and a poor one, less than 30kg. To put these figures in perspective, it takes about 10kg of opium to produce one kilogram of heroin. The 2006 harvest equates to some 4100 tons – worth an estimated 2.7 billion dollars US.

Afghan poppy.

'Of course we're growing poppy this year,' said a district chief. 'The government, the foreigners – they promised us help if we stopped. But where is it?'

Dusting with Agent Orange. In all, some 12 million gallons of this substance were dropped over Vietnam.

THE SOLUTIONS?

In late 2006, America declared that it was going to mount an all-out war on poppy cultivation in 2007; but at the time of writing, no set strategy had been agreed. One proposal on the table recommends airborne spraying of all known poppy fields with chemical agents. Understandably, this idea has been met with great concern in some quarters, as it smacks of the highly controversial Vietnam-era Operation Ranch Hand. For those who don't remember, this was an operation in which American aircraft sprayed a chemical defoliant agent called Agent Orange (so-called because of the colour of the barrels it was supplied in) over suspected VC positions and

'We need the British to stop the smugglers' – Governor Sher Mohammed Akhunzada

supply routes under the jungle canopy. The agent, made by Monsanto, did indeed work as predicted, clearing the jungle, but it had serious side effects that are still a very sensitive issue in the US military even today. Many soldiers developed terminal cancers as a consequence of their exposure to it, to say nothing of the Vietnamese beneath the poisonous deluge. Other options include mounting search and destroy missions. Again, highly controversial and difficult, as many of the drug barons have their own private, well-equipped armies. NATO has enough gunmen to contend with already, without adding even more elements to the tactical equation.

To give you some idea of the typical size of an Afghan drug-dealing operation, one dealer, Mansur Khan, employs some 300 people, many of whom are armed with heavy machine guns and RPGs. Operating from a heavily defended luxury compound, he has a large fleet of well-equipped pick-up trucks and land cruisers that he employs for narcotics trafficking throughout Afghanistan. In his particular case, most of the product is sold in neighbouring Iran. The methods of trafficking vary from job to job, some involving 4x4s, some horses, bikes, and on occasions even rafts. Moving a narcotics convoy through Afghanistan is no easy task, as rival drug dealers often try and hijack product from others to avoid cultivation and purchasing costs themselves. There is also the matter of paying bribes to police and government officials to turn a blind eye. Corruption is rife in this part of the world. Once the pockets of authority are lined, convoys move in two packets – one for checking the route out ahead of the main group, and the other for carrying the product itself. In case of problems or compromise, decoy and alternative routes are preplanned. It is a mini military

Soldiers of the New Zealand Army prepare to burn opium as part of a reconstruction effort in Afghanistan. Although small in number, they have played a major role in operations since 9/11, especially during the Tora Bora campaign, where the NZ SAS engaged in heavy actions in the cave complexes that dominated this area.

operation. For an Afghan narcotics dealer, the worst case scenario is running into either a NATO patrol or an Afghan one, as they will both put you into custody.

Other, less risky strategies for persuading dealers and farmers to quit the poppy trade include the British idea of refurbishing old, decommissioned Western tractors for use in Afghanistan by poor farmers. This project is in fact under way right now and is achieving some success. This project was first rolled out in Helmand Province – the number one opium poppy producing region in the country. This is one way of cutting back on the enormous amount of money that is currently finding its way into the Taliban's coffers through the narcotics trade. For the Afghan government, and outside foreign agencies, Helmand is the COG (Centre of Gravity) of the opium business. Its collapse, if well handled, could cause a domino effect throughout the country. In support of this strategy is a controversial idea to actually buy the opium poppy at market rates and then destroy it. This proposal has much going for it, as it would considerably cut back on narcotics entering the West and at the same time, keep dealers and farmers onside until a more profitable legal commodity can be farmed in Afghanistan. The seductively crazy logic of such an idea shows how intractable the situation is.

There are signs, albeit small ones, that some changes are taking place in the mindset of the Afghan people over the trade. These changes are in part being encouraged by local elders and tribal heads who are requesting their farmers not to sow opium poppy in the future. And that has to be good news for Afghanistan. Especially so, as only recently UK Prime Minister Tony Blair admitted that his government had very little to show for six years of effort against the crop since the fall of the Taliban.

Many of the Afghan people intuit that the West is only interested in the opium problem because of the effects it has on their own society, rather than that of the Afghan people. It is a fair point, and one that needs to be addressed as a matter of urgency. The Afghan people do accept that the British Army is trying very hard to bring peace and stability to the Helmand Province and that they are as frustrated as the Afghan people over the lack of obvious progress, particularly in terms of road building and utility restoration. Such programmes will bring work to the region and therefore lessen the dependency on opium cultivation.

Helmand is supposed to have received $55,000,000 US in alternative livelihood development aid in 2005, according to the UN's drugs control agency. This equates to some $55 per person in the Province – almost a quarter of an average person's annual income. However, there is very little evidence to suggest that the Province has received anywhere near as much money. Yes, there have been cash for work schemes – such as employing people on ditch draining projects and land tilling – but they do not pay anywhere near enough money to compensate for the loss of opium revenue. There is also the problem of farmers being indebted to the local drug barons and having no other methods of raising money, save for that of cultivating the poppy.

Both British and American anti-narcotics agencies admit that solving Afghanistan's opium problem will be a long and hard battle and that the issues of compensation for farmers stopping poppy cultivation need to be readdressed. This should in theory be a fair quid pro quo arrangement – but it's obvious that there are serious inconsistencies and shortfalls. Complying with President Hamid Karzai's edicts to stop growing poppy 'was explicitly seen as conditional on rapid compensation and rural development', states a European Union-funded study about the links between Afghanistan's opium economy and the conflict there, and it was in fact partly at the request of President Karzai that the US did not go ahead and spray the 2002 crop. There are many who

Burning balls of opium resin.

feel that the pressure should shift onto the traffickers and Mr Bigs of the opium trade and away from the farmers; many of them are involuntarily involved, coerced by death threats from the Taliban and Al-Qaeda. (Interestingly, a small number of detainees at Guantanamo Bay, from Iran and Yemen, claim not to be terrorists, but present in Afghanistan as participants in the drug trade.)

Dealing with Afghanistan's opium trade since the fall of the Taliban has not been one of the West's finest moments – and much more clearly needs to be done to help the Afghan people to build alternative livelihoods. As one Afghan official put it: 'Dealing with the drug problem has been a failure – a failure that soaks into every aspect of the country's progress.'

B1 with JDAMs.

The iconic B-52. Often it is older than the pilots flying it.

V

Hell from Above

In modern conflict, everyone knows that air power is a critical component of military strategy. It is almost always necessary, but not necessarily always decisive. However, in Afghanistan at the beginning it was both necessary *and* decisive. Having seen the devastating effect that air power had on the Iraqi forces during the first Gulf War of 1991, the US has been a keen proponent of the dictum that air power rules over everything else on the battlefield; this despite its obvious failure during the Kosovo conflict of 1991, where air power alone had little effect on the Serbian forces deployed. Afghanistan, however, was to be a different story. In this conflict, air power was cleverly orchestrated by ground-based special forces and CIA operatives, who through patient, diligent and highly dangerous work, marked out targets for the bombers and strike aircraft that were flying high above them, making them a lethal combination. In this war, the mighty, iconic B-52 was used as a close support aircraft, rather than a strategic bomber, a concept that would have been laughed at during the Vietnam War. But in this conflict it worked. With the ability to fly for hours at a time over suspected Taliban positions the B-52 was a greatly feared weapon. It gave special forces on the ground constant, instant, lethal firepower. The Taliban, in their fixed, exposed trench positions high above on the mountain ridges were sitting ducks.

During the first few weeks of the air campaign in Afghanistan, the heavy bombers, the B1, B2 and B-52, were

A C-130 Hercules of the New Zealand Air Force blasts off from a remote airstrip. All serve as part of Operation Concord.

Danger: low-flying Kiwis. A New Zealand Herc banks over a New Zealand FOB in Bamian Province.

in great demand. But with the gradual demise of set targets and installations, bombers were phased out and replaced with close-support aircraft such as the A-10, F-16, F-18 and of course the mighty AC-130 Spectre gunship, the only active fixed-wing gunship in the world. This aircraft is a favourite amongst special forces as it has extremely sophisticated sensors that can be used for detecting both vehicle and human movement. For local close support, tactical planners prefer using attack helicopters such as the Apache, rather than strike aircraft, as they have greater loiter capability and therefore more deterrent value. This is really important during high tempo operations, such as those being fought in Helmand Province at the time of writing, where the Taliban will lie low when a close support aircraft is around, knowing full well it cannot remain on station long, whereas an Apache can hover miles away from the action, yet still be on hand for support, without the Taliban even being aware of its presence.

Mission tasking is usually local to the forces being supported, with target designation carried out by a suitably qualified fire control officer. I say this, as on occasions, American pilots have refused to accept instructions from non officers, whereas for British forces air support can be called in by anyone qualified – be it officer or NCO. The Americans' caution is understandable, in the light of the many incidents where mistakes have been made by personnel calling in air support that resulted in catastrophic friendly-fire losses. In most of these tragic cases, the victims were fellow Americans, but in others, they were allies. One such incident caused the deaths of four Canadian soldiers, leading to bad feeling between Canadian and American armed forces in the country at the time. Feelings were intensified when it was discovered that the F-16 pilot responsible for the fratricide had been refused permission to initiate an attack and yet still went ahead. In another fatal mistake, an AC-130 Spectre gunship (Grim 31) strafed an American special forces convoy as it was en route to participate in Operation Anaconda. The incident resulted from a navigation and communications error, with no blame being apportioned to the crew or the victims concerned.

Another mishap occurred when a special forces team requested a recce of an area ahead of their line of advance. Upon hearing this, the aircraft tasked with the mission flew ahead of the ground force concerned and carpet bombed the area. It transpired that they had misunderstood the request: they thought that they had been instructed to 'to wreck the area ahead'. Thankfully on this occasion there was no damage, except to one aircrew's pride. Mistakes get made in warfare, everyone accepts that. But to lose a colleague to friendly fire just seems that much harder to bear, as there is always the feeling that it could all have been avoided.

Targeting mistakes, collateral damage – or spillage as the Americans now call it – is a serious issue. In general, targets identified by ground based units are far less likely to result in collateral damage: the MK One eyeball method is pretty sound and reliable. That is unless a bomb goes rogue, which does happen from time to time. Another targeting method in the Afghan air war is the placing of targeting strobes around suspected Taliban positions by friendly Afghans. When this tactic works, it works real well, as the locals know who is who and can spot an outsider a mile away. There are however two down-sides to this practice. The first one is that if the Afghan is actually a Taliban sympathiser rather than a friendly, he may place the infra-red (IR) targeting strobe near the dwelling of an innocent family, thereby causing civilian casualties and a backlash against NATO. The second complication is personal motive. Sometimes Afghans with a grudge against fellow Afghans will allege that they are Taliban, and then have them targeted. In southern Afghanistan a farmer owed a local loan shark money. The farmer placed a strobe on the roof of his house. One JDAM later: debt cancelled.

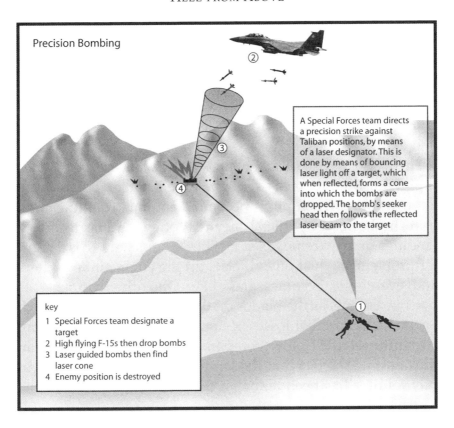

Precision Bombing

A Special Forces team directs a precision strike against Taliban positions, by means of a laser designator. This is done by means of bouncing laser light off a target, which when reflected, forms a cone into which the bombs are dropped. The bomb's seeker head then follows the reflected laser beam to the target

key

1 Special Forces team designate a target
2 High flying F-15s then drop bombs
3 Laser guided bombs then find laser cone
4 Enemy position is destroyed

Harrier ready for action in Afghanistan.

For many soldiers in Afghanistan, air support is a lifeline. It is generally accepted that 60 soldiers in helicopters are worth 600 soldiers in vehicles. As in Vietnam, the helicopter is the preferred method of transport. Helo operations in Afghanistan however, can be extremely demanding, both of man and machine. The hot and high conditions limit range and load.

Dust is a major problem, it wrecks blades and engines rapidly and sometimes even whole helicopters. It can cause a brown out – when pilots become disorientated and cannot find the horizon by visual means – often leading to heavy landings or in extreme cases, crashes. Engine failure is a regular problem, as dust often blocks up the engine intake filters and eventually becomes glass-like. Once this happens, its bye bye engine, as the blades on the jet spool will be trashed. Surprisingly, combat losses of helicopters in Afghanistan are currently relatively low compared to those in Iraq, so far. This despite the fact that the tempo of military operations in this country has been amongst the most intensive since the Korean War.

Helicopters serve three principal roles in Afghanistan: attack, support and tactical reconnaissance. In the attack role, they provide direct close support during operations, supply helicopter escort, and top cover for vulnerable convoys. It is, however, in the support role that they really come into their own, as they move everything, from bulldozers to bullets, soldiers and supplies. In the reconnaissance role, they observe potential targets and suspected Taliban positions to mark them out for attack from ground or air.

GERONIMO: APACHES GO TO WAR

In Afghanistan, the principal attack helicopter used by the British, American and Dutch forces is the Apache. This has been an outstanding success during ground support operations and is the platform of choice for close support. It can

Two Apaches provide escort for an RAF Chinook. Although impressive in performance, these helicopters urgently need more effective weaponry against mud-walled compounds and caves, as current cannons, rockets and Hellfire missiles are not proving lethal enough against these types of targets. As a result, the UK MoD is looking to procure thermobaric weaponry, but is concerned that its use may infringe human rights.

hover over a target and rain down lead, or rockets, as and when required. A close support aircraft has to constantly over-fly the target again and again to achieve anything. Even though many NATO allies operate the Apache, the tactics of choice vary from one country to another. For instance, in US use they carry full ammunition loads during operations, which gives them less time on station, whereas in British hands they carry barely a third of the helicopter's 30mm cannon capacity preferring to carry more fuel instead. This means that during a fire support mission they tend to fire short, six-round bursts at a target, using the cannon as a precision sniping weapon. With the Apache's excellent night vision capability, this makes for a highly efficient kill system.

At present, the UK has eight Apaches operating in Afghanistan, four at Kandahar, and four at the forward operational base of Camp Bastion, where at any given time, two Apaches and two Chinooks are always on stand-by for QRF (Quick Reaction Force) duties and Casevac. All British Apaches are from 9 Regiment in Dishforth, North Yorkshire, who rotate crews between the Regiment's two squadrons, 656 and 664. Both units have seen significant action, with some Apaches involved in as many as four combat missions a day. From August to November 2006 they clocked 2,147 hours of operational flying, firing 9,100 30mm rounds, 65 CRV-7 rockets and 28 AGM-114 Hellfire missiles. In addition to direct troop support operations, the Apaches also ride shotgun for ground convoys and other air missions. On some occasions, they also carry out pre-fires – armed reconnaissance missions, usually carried out in advance of a ground offensive.

At this time, there is a great deal of pressure being put on the UK MoD by both the Army and Air Force to provide a new type of dedicated reconnaissance helicopter, equipped with the highly capable Broadsword system. Although this operational demand has generated a lot of interest, in the short term, it is unlikely to happen, as the UK has a major shortfall in support helicopters – both in Afghanistan and Iraq – and this need is far more pressing.

One particularly interesting aspect of British Apache operation is the fact that the crew can self-designate targets, for themselves or others, because as at least one crew member is always airborne forward air controller (Ab-FAC)-qualified. This is a highly valuable skill-set, minimising the risk of friendly fire incidents: one of the reasons why many other NATO forces operating in Afghanistan like working alongside the British. One other tactic used by the British pilots to great effect is the use by the Apache crew of night vision goggles (NVGs) to view targets designated by ground troops using laser pointers. It's very crude – but it works really well.

For personal protection, each Apache crew member carries both a pistol and a short barrelled SA-80A2 assault rifle. In addition, they also carry a sat phone, as the helicopter is only equipped with line of sight radios and in the mountainous regions of Afghanistan, this can make communications a problem.

Recently, the importance of the Apache was summed up by Sir Jock Stirrup, the Chief of Defence Staff: 'The Apache has, over the course of 2006, established itself, with friend and foe alike, as one of our most powerful and flexible weapon systems, as a battle-winning capability.'

THE JETS

In Afghanistan at present, fast jet close support is provided by American A-10s and F/A-18s, Dutch F-16s, French Mirage 2000s and British Harriers; all with their own strengths and weaknesses. For loitering time, the American A-10 is a firm favourite with the ground troops. It can carry a massive weapons load, including its formidable 30mm Gatling-Gun. And it can take enormous punishment. For speed, the F/A-18s, Mirages and F-16s cannot be beaten, plus they offer the capability of all-weather operation. The jack of all trades is the Harrier: an aircraft that is capable of vertical take-off and landing, hovering, flying sideways, and even backwards. But in Afghanistan it does not perform any of these tricks; life out there is no flying circus. Although the RAF only has seven of these aircraft in-theatre, they get around, and are particularly popular with US special forces, following an operation in which the Harrier pilots saved American soldiers from Taliban fighters who were threatening to overrun their defensive position.

That sentiment, however, is not shared by some members of the British Army, who have expressed the opinion that the RAF has been totally useless in supporting them. This was a particularly hard criticism for the brave pilots putting their lives on the line, as they, with the best will in the world, cannot be everywhere. Operating out of Kandahar Airfield, the Harrier GR.7As of Joint Harrier Force (JHF) Sqn are certainly busy, having being involved in record numbers of sorties since British forces first entered Helmand Province. Now tasked with providing a 24-hour tactical footprint, they are working flat out in all weathers and all conditions, placing great pressure on their pilots. Not only do they get fired at in the air, but frequently their base at Kandahar gets attacked, often leaving aircraft damaged.

Another issue the British pilots have is with the fidelity of their Thermal Imaging Aircraft Laser Designator (TIALD) which is just not accurate enough for them to discern all targets presented to them during high tempo close support operations. However, the American Litening II pod can overcome this problem. The British are keen to acquire a capability like this, as it will enable a better battle picture to be presented to both the pilots and ground forces during complicated engagements. Litening provides an FLIR with three fields of view, a CCD camera for daytime performance, a 100mJ laser designator; and, uniquely, a laser spot designator that can detect laser energy from a secondary source – allowing ground or airborne FACs to designate the target.

The fast jets are called in when a precision strike is necessary, or a bigger punch is required than can be provided by the Apaches. Usually, this takes the form of either 500lb or 1000lb precision guided bombs, depending on target and proximity of friendly forces.

DANGER CLOSE

When dropping these types of bombs, considerable thought, unsurprisingly, must be given to the safety margins. Communication and coordination must be spot on and where possible a Forward Air Controller (FAC) should direct attacks. When operating in close proximity to an enemy, the term 'danger close' is often used. For each weapon used there is a certain blast hemisphere, and if you are inside it, you are in danger. For example, a 1000lb (454kg) bomb has a safety distance of around 3,280 ft (1000m). Obviously, the closer you are to the epicentre of the explosion, the higher your personal risk. If friendly forces are within the ring of death, a danger close warning will be issued by the pilot. If they are willing to accept this risk – he will release ordnance. However, it is not uncommon during high-tempo operations for bombs to be dropped within 1,000ft of friendly forces; and there have even been cases where some Allied troops have been within 500ft (150m) of a bomb's impact zone.

B1 dropping bombs.

Dick Cheney at the opening of the Afghan Parliament, 19 December 2005. Only recently in 2007 an attempt was made on his life at Bagram Air Base.

'We will succeed in Iraq, just like we did in Afghanistan.'

Dick Cheney, 23 June 2005

VI

Chariots of the Damned

I once used this title for a book that I co-authored some years ago with Major Mike McKinney, of the USAF Special Operations Group (SOG), because I felt that it summed up the stories of the brave pilots and aircrew that were featured within it. This time around, I'm using it again because one of the pilots that I interviewed for this book told me his aircrew buddies chalked the title of my book on the nose of their Chinook: it just reflected their feelings at the time about how operations were going for their squadron during their tour of duty in Afghanistan. As you have probably guessed, I have great personal admiration for the pilots and aircrew who serve in Afghanistan, as they get little praise or recognition for the work they do in supporting the ground forces that are battling for Afghanistan's future. To me, the images of Chinooks blasting up dust clouds as they ride into the bedlam that is Helmand Province are just as iconic as those of the Huey over Vietnam. Here are the stories of a few of these brave men.

COURAGE AND LOSS ON TAKUR GHAR

March 2, 2002: the American-led Operation Anaconda – the thrust that is going to push the Taliban and Al-Qaeda fighters out of the Shahi-Kot Valley once and for all – is just not going to plan. The opposition is far stronger than was envisaged. Fearing a calamity as the casualties continued to mount, American senior commanders ordered SEAL teams (Mako 21 and Mako 30) onto the high ridge of Takur Ghar, an impressive feature that gave a commanding viewpoint of all the surrounding valleys, including the Shahi-Kot. Eyes up there should give them an edge in this tough battle, as they could spot and anticipate Taliban and Al-Qaeda tactical movements long in advance of them becoming a threat. It made good sense of course. But if the Americans thought it was a key position, then surely the guerrilla fighters thought that also? So an aerial reconnoitring of the peak was sanctioned in advance of the SEAL's insertion. This task went to AC-130 Spectre gunship (Nail 22), who declared the area clear and safe within minutes of the air tasking order.

Satisfied that all was well, the SEALs boarded two Night Stalker Chinooks – Razor 03 and Razor 04 – and proceeded towards the peak of Takur Ghar. This however, had not been their original intention. They had hoped to be dropped 1300 metres east of the peak the previous day, and from there make their way covertly towards the peak before dawn. But one of

US Night Stalkers keep their eyes peeled for Taliban activity.

their rides was unserviceable, so a replacement helicopter had to be found; hence the delay. It was now almost 0245 hours on March 4 – and as Razor 03 began to flare over the LZ of Takur Ghar, disaster struck. From out of the blackness of the night there was a series of bright flashes as machine guns opened up on them from all sides, culminating with an RPG impacting on the left side electrical compartment of the Chinook's cargo bay, causing it to judder briefly. As the stricken helicopter struggled to get airborne out of harm's way, Petty Officer First Class Neil Roberts slipped on some hydraulic fluid that had leaked from the damaged helicopter, causing him to fall off the rear ramp and plummet onto the deep snow that covered the peak.

Quickly realising they had a man overboard, the crew tried to swing the Chinook around to pick him up, but could not do so as the controls had locked up. This meant leaving him behind to an almost certain death. By now the crew were fighting for their own survival as the helicopter was losing height rapidly, leaving them with no choice but to crash-land on the valley floor below, some four miles away from Roberts. Once out of the helicopter they were soon joined on the ground by the second Chinook, Razor 04, which had been out of contact with them due to radio failure, which is why they had not been together on the peak. Their first thoughts were to get straight back up onto the peak and rescue Roberts, but this was not possible. First, Razor 04 could not take them all in one lift, owing to the altitude at which they were now operating. Second, they could not leave anyone behind with the crashed helicopter, as Al-Qaeda fighters were already closing in fast on them from across the valley. So with heavy hearts they left Roberts behind and headed back to their base at Gardez.

Once there, they quickly dropped off Razor 04's crew and immediately returned to the Takur Ghar peak to search for Roberts. While at Gardez, they picked up an extra passenger, air controller, Air Force Tech. Sgt. John A. Chapman, as they knew

The remains of Chinook Razor 01 on top of Takur Ghar.

things were likely to get pretty hot on that ridge. By now, all hell
was breaking loose in HQ command at Bagram air base, outside
Kabul as they tried to make some sense of the tactical picture
at Takur Ghar – and find out what had become of Roberts. Air
tasking officers immediately tried to divert an aircraft over the
peak, but none was available. That was the key reason for this
mission's failure: had a gunship been available to make a last-
minute surveillance sweep or pre-fire of the LZ prior to Razor
03's arrival, then maybe the whole sorry mess would not have
occurred. However, the story does not end there.

Just prior to Razor 04's arrival back at the peak, both an
AC-130 gunship and a Predator UAV reported seeing Roberts
moving around the LZ, engaging Al-Qaeda fighters with his
M-249 SAW (Squad Automatic Weapon). Although encourag-
ing news at first, it did not last for long. His weapon jammed,
leading to his capture and subsequent death, possibly
execution.

This information was not relayed to Razor 04 as it began to flare for a hot landing near Roberts' last known position. Normally, it would have been standard and prudent practice to hose the LZ down with heavy, withering fire, to keep the heads of the enemy down. But fearing that they might hit Roberts, the crew declined to do this. As the Chinook hovered above the ground, machine-guns opened up on them from all sides, raking the helicopter from bow to stern. The pilot, who had never flown into a hot combat zone before, had his baptism of fire. He rapidly disgorged the air controller and SEAL team of Mako 30 into the maelstrom. There were hidden fire positions all around them, leaving them with only one option: to charge one of the positions, which was in a trench under some trees. As they charged, they fired directly at the trench, killing two Al-Qaeda fighters. A hidden enemy bunker spotted them and opened fire, mortally wounding Chapman and injuring two of the SEALs as they engaged. Realising they were in an indefensible killing zone, the SEALs moved off the peak into better cover on the northeast side of the mountain. As they did this, an AC-130 Spectre gunship (Grim 32) provided covering fire with its Gatling guns, 40mm cannon, and 105mm airborne howitzer.

As dawn broke, a Quick Reaction Force (QRF), consisting of a JTAC controller, a three-man USAF special tactics team and a force of 19 Rangers under the command of Capt. Nathan Self were scrambled from their base at Bagram in two Chinooks – Razor 01 and Razor 02 – in support of the SEALs. Acting upon only the most sketchy information, the Rangers headed for the SEALs' position, to link up and extract. As Self later pointed out: 'A quick reaction force is never going to know everything that's going on. If they did, then they wouldn't be quick.' True enough, but that lack of information now saw him heading for the SEALs' original LZ on the peak itself, and not their new location. As they neared the mountain, Razor 02 commenced a wagon wheel holding pattern, providing some top cover, while Self in Razor 01 flared for a landing. It was just as well, as barely had Razor 01 touched down when it was hit in the right engine by an RPG, quickly followed by bursts of machine-gun fire. One of Razor 01's forward gunners, Sgt. Philip J. Svitak, returned fire with his 7.62mm machine gun, but was soon struck and killed by the overwhelming incoming enemy fire. Shortly after, the other forward gunner was hit and wounded, along with the two pilots, who both staggered from the now-burning Chinook.

As the remaining members of the QRF darted out from the carcass of Razor 01, three of their number – Private First Class Matt Commons, Sergeant Brad Crose, and Specialist Marc Anderson – were killed by the murderous incoming fire that was now impacting all around the LZ, leaving only a few brave and wounded men to continue the fight. By this time, Razor 02 had returned to the crash site after having been temporarily diverted away to Gardez bringing with it the rest of the QRF. With their arrival and that of close air support, the position was consolidated and secured.

This temporary respite did not last for long. The Al-Qaeda and Taliban forces launched an all out counter-attack. At the height of these attacks, bombs were being dropped 'danger close' all around the LZ, as the only way in which to prevent it from being overrun. Despite fantastic efforts by all concerned, another US casualty was sustained; Senior Airman Jason D. Cunningham, a para-rescue combat medic, was mortally wounded.

If any of the brave men that day should be singled out for special mention, then surely it must Cunningham. The words selfless hero seem woefully inadequate. Despite being in agony from his own wounds, he refused morphine, as it would inhibit his medical judgement while helping the others that lay around him. Even in his dying moments, he continued to give medical advice to the Rangers, so that they could continue saving their fellow countrymen, as he knew a medevac was impossible in broad daylight.

A US Army Chinook flies down an Afghan canyon so as to avoid a possible ambush.

Eventually, after what would seem a lifetime for most, they were extracted. They left behind 200 dead Al-Qaeda and Taliban fighters as proof of America's most intense military action since the infamous 'Blackhawk Down' incident in Mogadishu in 1993. They are all a credit to the military of the United States. Both Technical Sergeant Chapman and Senior Airman Cunningham were awarded the Air Force Cross, the second highest award for bravery in the United States.

DIGGERS IN THE DIRT

There were some other heroes in attendance that day that nobody speaks of, as very few knew they were there. I refer to the Australian Special Air Service Regiment (SASR). They, unbeknown to most, had infiltrated the Taliban lines around the Shahi-Kot valley with the intention of setting up an observation post that could provide intelligence for Operation

Anaconda. But by sheer good fortune, it was in sight of Takur Ghar also. As a result, the Australians had seen the entire saga unfold and were able to provide continuous intel for the calling in and directing of air strikes around the ill fated American LZ. In recognition of their excellent work. The commander of the SASR in Afghanistan was awarded the US Bronze Star for his unit's outstanding performance.

FLIGHT OF THE PHOENIX

One other story, which I found utterly amazing, unfolded in January 2007. Two Apache helicopters carrying four Royal Marines strapped upon their fuselage were involved in a spectacular rescue operation to recover a fallen comrade. When I first heard about it, I felt both great admiration for the soldiers and aircrew involved and yet at the same time anger as to why they had to resort to such a crude method of insertion, when we had purpose-built special forces insertion/extraction pods that could have been used instead. These gave full protection from small calibre rounds. I know this because I headed up the design team that developed the Avpro Exint, special forces pod system, in anticipation of just such a scenario. As for the men who bravely D-ringed themselves onto the fuselage sides in a manner reminiscent of that seen in the movie, *Flight of the Phoenix* – one can only praise their outstanding courage.

The mission became necessary after a failed Royal Marine-led assault on the Taliban-held Jugroom Fort, in Garmser, southern Helmand. The riverside fort was a high-walled compound, ringed by watchtowers containing machine guns and RPGs. It had been the subject of a two-month surveillance operation. It was believed that high-ranking Taliban leaders were using it as a command HQ, so it was felt more appropriate to assault it rather than simply bomb it, in order to preserve any valuable intelligence and documentation held within. Realising it was heavily defended, the British

A spectacular image of a British soldier riding in on an Apache during the Jugroom Fort incident. This photograph was provided by the Apache riding shotgun on the mission. Note: all information data has been obscured for OPSEC reasons.

assaulted in strength, with a force of some 200 commandos drawn from 45 Commando, backed up by heavily armed Viking armoured vehicles and Scimitar light tanks, covered from above by Apaches.

In theory, it should have been a relatively straightforward assault but within minutes of the get-go, four soldiers were wounded after coming under a hail of withering fire. A re-org was called. It was during this reassessment that it became apparent the marines were a man down; and that they would need to go back and find him. The use of Vikings was quickly ruled out as they were deemed too slow and vulnerable. There had to be another option. It was at this point that an Apache pilot put forward the idea of mounting a rescue mission by means of the Apaches assigned in support of the original assault. All Apache aircrew are familiar with the theory of such a rescue, as it is a recognized procedure for recovering downed aircrew. The only problem was that nobody in the British forces had ever performed it for real. So it would be a first for all concerned.

After agreeing it could be performed, four Royal Marines quickly stepped forward as volunteers, anxious to recover their fellow marine, Lance Corporal Matthew Ford. Once briefed, they attached themselves to the Apaches and took off towards the fort, with the pilots keeping the speed down so as not to buffet them against the fuselage. Each Apache involved in the rescue carried two soldiers – one each side of the cockpit, while the third helicopter rode shotgun. As they approached the fort they came under fire but this was quickly suppressed, by both the helicopters themselves and supporting ground forces. Taking advantage of this firepower, the

A Royal Marine mortar observer at Kajaki.

two Apaches landed near a compound wall – where they had seen the fallen soldier's still body.

All four Commandos got off and hurriedly recovered it back to the Apaches, while one of the Apache pilots gave covering fire. Just as quickly as they had arrived they were gone in a cloud of dust, leaving the Taliban somewhat bewildered as to what they had just witnessed. Alas, their extraordinary efforts had sadly been in vain. Lance Corporal Ford was already dead from his injuries.

It was a bitter blow, but at least they had got him back. Paying tribute, his commanding officer, Lieutenant Colonel Duncan Dewar, described his fallen soldier thus: 'Lance Corporal Ford was a popular and gregarious young Royal Marine whose professionalism, reliability, and selflessness, as well as his sharp wit, marked him out from the crowd.'

CITATIONS

As you can imagine, there have been hundreds of missions flown in Afghanistan since 9/11 that warrant description. Some (and some I am aware of) cannot be revealed. Some can, and are now public knowledge. These include the missions that led to the official citations for service personnel serving with the RAF in Afghanistan read out during the award ceremony in 2006, which honoured their supreme courage and bravery. A Squadron Leader, a Flight Lieutenant, a Flying Officer and a Royal Marine Major attached to the RAF have all received the Distinguished Flying Cross for their conspicuous bravery in Afghanistan. In addition, 11 other RAF personnel were honoured at the Ministry of Defence at the same time for their service around the world, principally in Iraq and Afghanistan.

Two soldiers from the 3rd Battalion the Parachute Regiment were posthumously honoured with the highest gallantry awards for their exceptional valour. One received a Victoria Cross and the other a George Cross. Defence Secretary Des

Browne said: 'In Iraq, Afghanistan and across the world our brave men and women continue to put their lives on the line in the pursuit of security and stability. They are an inspiration to us all.' Chief of the Defence Staff, Air Chief Marshal Sir Jock Stirrup said: 'The past year has been one of great challenge for the people of our armed forces, and they have consistently delivered above and beyond our already high expectation. I am immensely proud of them all; and these honours reflect the nation's pride.'

In addition to the four DFCs, the Military Cross was awarded to Flt Lt Matthew Carter of the RAF Regiment. His 'selfless bravery' as a forward air controller in Afghanistan was critical in destroying Taliban positions. The DFC was awarded to Royal Marine Major Mark Hammond for his actions in three engagements in southern Afghanistan in September 2006. Flying a Chinook helicopter as an exchange pilot with 18(Bomber) Sqn from RAF Odiham, Major Hammond rescued three separate casualties in one night, each time in the face of heavy enemy fire. DFCs were also awarded to Harrier pilot Sqn Ldr John Monahan and Chinook pilots Flt Lt Craig Wilson and FO Christopher Hasler. Mentioned in Dispatches were Sqn Ldr Michael Woods, Sgt Graham Jones and Daniel Baxter and Flt Lt Warren Keenan. The Queen's Commendation for Valuable Service (QCVS) was awarded to Air Cdre Barry North OBE, Gp Capt Malcolm Brecht OBE, Wg Cdr Richard Clifford, and Sqn Ldrs Derek Watson and Robin Norman.

Sqn Ldr John Mason was a pilot with the Joint Force Harrier Detachment, part of 904 Expeditionary Air Wing at Kandahar. On 24 April 2006, he was due to fly a two-Harrier patrol providing Close Air Support for ground forces. Prior to take off the second Harrier developed a problem and Monahan decided to go solo. Within a few minutes 'on station' he received a transmission from Australian forces who were under sustained attack by the Taliban, pinned down, unable to retreat and running out of ammunition. Normally they

Royal Marines check-fire their weapons prior to a mission.

would be required to mark their position so the Harrier could identify the enemy but did not because they feared that in doing so they would give away their position more clearly to the enemy and be overrun. Monahan decided to descend from the relative safety of higher altitude and made low level passes to establish the position of enemy forces, each time through effective and sustained fire from the ground. In doing so he managed to pinpoint the Taliban and drop munitions, which silenced the guns with direct hits, allowing the Australians to retreat without any casualties, re-arm and continue their patrol. His composure, in the full sight of the enemy and under the most intense pressure, undoubtedly saved the lives of numerous Australian troops in what was a selfless act of commitment, and total mission focus. He was awarded the DFC.

Flt Lt Craig Wilson was Captain of a Chinook from 1310 Flt in Helmand Province. On 11 June 2006 he was tasked with his second casualty evacuation of the day. He had only been in-theatre a few weeks and had completed a minimum of theatre night flying. A British soldier had been very seriously injured during enemy contact. To avoid giving away his presence and maximising the element of surprise, he flew at 150ft and landed with precision at night in the middle of the stranded patrol's location, recovering the man to safety. Just a few hours later he was tasked yet again with a casevac, but had to hold off while an Apache gunship suppressed enemy action. By the time he returned to base with the casualty he had barely enough fuel to remain airborne, but he knew a man's life had been at stake. Gallantry and extreme and persistent courage ensured the recovery of the two very seriously wounded British soldiers and almost certainly played a vital role in saving their lives. A short while later he volunteered to fly another mission – despite having been on duty 22 hours – to insert troops badly needed as re-enforcements. He was awarded the DFC.

Flying Officer Christopher Hasler was a Chinook Captain, also part of 1310 Flt. In July 2006, as a relatively inexperienced pilot, he led a formation of Chinooks into Sangin, a Taliban stronghold, to re-supply and extract elements of 3 Para, under extremely dangerous conditions. The day before a soldier had been killed trying to secure the helicopter landing site. To make the most of surprise he chose to land in an area away from the usual landing site, where there were buildings on three sides, with the ever present threat of one of the two rotors striking a building and causing catastrophic damage. To give the Chinook more space he intentionally calculated to land with the spinning rotors passing above a single-storey rooftop. Any error could have been fatal. The mission was a complete success. On another occasion he landed troops while the Taliban were firing at him with RPGs and rifles. He held his nerve while his troops were disembarking at the hottest of landing sites, allowing them to suppress enemy positions with minimum British casualties. He acted with great courage and composure in the most demanding, high-risk environment the Chinook Force has operated in within recent

In November 2006, 2 Para was just 48 hours away from doing this over Afghanistan. This stemmed from the fears over UK platoon houses being over-run in Helmand province.

Royal Marines of 3 Commando prepare to extract from Now Zad.

history and displayed the highest standards of gallantry and professionalism, together with outstanding capability as a helicopter captain. He was awarded the DFC.

RM Major Mark Hammond was an exchange Chinook pilot with 19(B) Sqn and was involved in three separate casevac engagements in one night in September 2006, during which he showed leadership, superior flying skills and inspirational command of his crew – each time under fire. The first was the extraction of a seriously wounded soldier from Sangin. While Apaches provided suppressing fire he made an aggressive, quick approach to the landing site and successfully collected the casualty. On arrival back at Camp Bastion he received a second call to extract a critical casualty. Despite knowing the casualty location was under attack from the Taliban, he landed using night vision goggles while being engaged by enemy fire from several positions. The approach had to be

3 Para along with other NATO units perform a sweep and clear operation at Sangin.

aborted. A nearby Apache crew witnessed two rocket propelled grenades (RPGs) pass just 10 metres above and below the Chinook. Back at base, four rounds were found to have hit the aircraft, one causing almost catastrophic damage to a wing blade root. So Hammond took another Chinook and, despite further sustained fire, managed to extract the badly injured soldier. He was awarded the DFC. He was also awarded the QCVS for his services during Op Telic (Iraq) in 2002.

RAF Regiment Flt Lt Matthew Carter was a Tactical Air Control Party officer within 3 PARA operating in southern Afghanistan. The RAF Regiment provides the vital links between ground forces and air power by directing air assets in response to events on the ground, including directing fire onto enemy ground positions. Carter regularly directed close and accurate attack helicopter fire with devastating results, neutralising the enemy with ruthless precision. In one firefight he left the protection of his vehicle and forced his way to the front line without regard for his personal safety. In another attack, the fire he directed from the air was on a Taliban target only 30 metres from his own position. But the risk was essential, given the ferocious weight of fire coming in, which would otherwise have resulted in significant casualties. In a further incident he was part of a force being dropped off at night to capture a high-value Taliban Leader. The Chinook pilot had to take off after just 20 seconds, with Carter still inside, due to sudden incoming fire. Without regard for himself, Carter jumped out of the Chinook from 15ft, landed in a ditch and instantly began directed fire onto Taliban positions. He gallantly and repeatedly imperilled himself during all contacts with the enemy at a very high risk of being killed. He was awarded the Military Cross.

Sqn Ldr Michael Woods was Officer Commanding 1310 Flt of Chinook Helicopters. Throughout his tour during the summer of 2006 he led high risk missions including troop insertion, which gave infantry the advantage of surprise, and

Moving kit at Camp Bastion.

Air force JTACs doing what they do best – calling in air strikes.

found himself under constant threats from Taliban ground positions. Attacks by an agile and determined enemy on platoon houses – temporary locations where soldiers base their operations – were on the increase and extraction of casualties under fire was frequently required. On arrival in theatre Woods galvanised all aspects of Chinook operations. The risk of aircraft being shot down remained extremely high throughout his tour and he also provided valuable moral support and guidance to his more inexperienced crews. He was mentioned in Dispatches.

Sgt Graham Jones was a Chinook crewman who showed the highest standards of professionalism, gallantry and airmanship during his ten-week deployment in Afghanistan as part of Operation Herrick. He was involved in a number of high-risk sorties and his actions were a constant source of inspiration to his fellow aviators. On 11 June 2006 he played a major role in the recovery of two British soldiers from two different landing sites, both under significant threat from enemy fire. The landings were made at night in dusty conditions with zero visibility. On another occasion, he landed 37 troops and a quad-bike into the Taliban heartland of Sangin. Suddenly the Chinook was engaged by RPG and small arms fire from both sides of the aircraft. Acting instinctively, Jones leapt from the aircraft and began firing at the enemy to provide cover for the quad to leave: not a required element of a crewman's duties. Once the quad was away he climbed aboard the Chinook and calmly continued with the take-off. He was Mentioned in Dispatches.

Sgt Daniel Baxter was a Chinook loadmaster and a crew member of the standby Chinook at Camp Bastion. On 6 September 2006 he acted with exceptional professionalism and bravery under enemy fire three times. The first was following a Taliban mortar attack on troops in Sangin and a casualty urgently needed uplifting from a platoon house. As they landed the Chinook came under fire and Jones returned fire from the helicopter as it took off, suppressing enemy fire to enable the casualty to be uplifted. On another occasion that day further casualties, including a seriously wounded soldier, required uplifting from Musa Qalah. Once again there was sustained enemy fire as they landed, as well as while returning to Camp Bastion. On later examination a number of bullet holes were found to have pierced the Chinook, and while engineers were working on the damage, a third call for urgent assistance was received and he boarded a second Chinook to retrieve more injured troops from Musa Qalah. Despite operating under fire three times and having 4 RPGs launched at his aircraft he showed professionalism and bravery under enemy fire. For his superb airmanship and situational awareness, Baxter was Mentioned in Dispatches.

Unlike in other conflicts, in which the US has been extremely generous in its recognition of the brave and courageous by means of copious medal awards and citations, Afghanistan and Iraq have in contrast been very constrained, muted affairs when it comes to the issuing of medals. This is despite years of bloody and intensive conflict, which has generated more than its fair share of heroes, in my view. They have largely gone unnoticed. One can only suspect that politicians are playing both conflicts down, so as to deflect public attention.

That said, there have been several notable exceptions where bravery and devotion to duty has been recognized by the US, and not only in their homegrown personnel. In 2002, six members of the British Special Boat Service received the Congressional Medal of Honor for outstanding bravery shown during the Qali-e-Jhangi fortress incident.

In recognition of outstanding courage displayed during the Takur Ghar incident of March 2 2002, three US servicemen were awarded with the following decorations. Tech Sgt John Chapman was posthumously awarded the Air Force Cross. Senior Airman Jason Cunningham was also posthumously awarded the Air Force Cross. His Citation states that he 'braved an intense small arms and rocket propelled

AFGHANISTAN

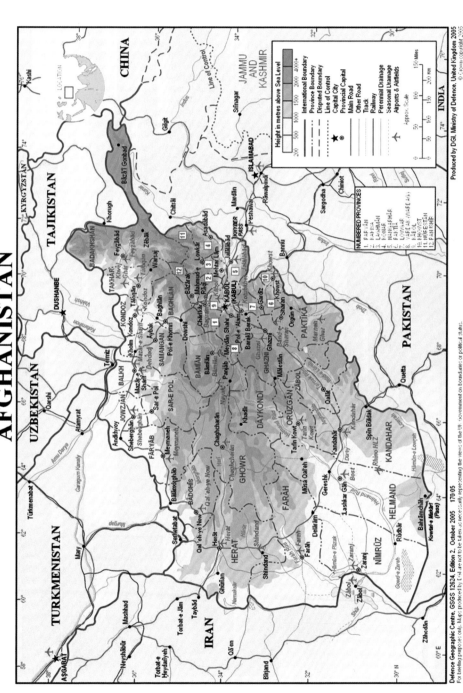

Height in metres above Sea Level

200	500	1000	1500	2000	3000	4000+

International Boundary
Province Boundary
Disputed Boundary
Line of Control
★ Capital City
◉ Provincial Capital
Main Road
Other Road
Track
Railway
Perennial Drainage
Seasonal Drainage
✈ Airports & Airfields

Approx. Scale

0   50   100   150 Miles
0   50   100   150   200 Km

NUMBERED PROVINCES
1. PARWAN
2. KAPISA
3. LAGHMAN
4. KONAR
5. NANGARHAR
6. PAKTIA
7. LOWGAR
8. WARDAK
9. KABUL
10. KHOWST
11. NORESTAN
12. PANSHIR

Defence Geographic Centre, GSGS 12624, Edition 2, October 2005   170-05

For briefing purpose only. Maps produced by DGI are not to be taken as necessarily representing the views of the UK government on boundaries or political status.

Produced by DGI, Ministry of Defence, United Kingdom 2005
© Crown copyright 2005

Above and left:
1 & 2. British SBS getting papped at the Qali-e-Jhangi fortress.

Right:
3. US Special Forces operator forcibly remonstrating with an Afghan.

4. Royal Marine with snatch Landrover. Note the lack of RPG cage protection and defensive weaponry.

5. Prime Minister Tony Blair with British troops at Camp Bastion, November 2006.

6. Royal Marines let rip with a .50 cal HMG during a contact at Now Zad.

⁷. Royal Marines under fire. Note the fixed bayonet mounted on the assault rifle of the marine giving situation report.

. Royal Marines open fire on Taliban positions with a 51mm mortar.

9. Operation Silica: Royal Marines go into all-around defence as their fellow commandos unload a Chinook. Engines and rotors are not shut down during these procedures.

10. Royal Marines extract from Now Zad during Operation Silica.

11. Soldiers from 3 Para prepare to storm a compound during Operation Snake Bite.

2. Alert 3 Para Soldier in an orchard during Operation Snake Bite.

13. An early Christmas present for the British forces serving in Afghanistan: the H & K 40mm grenade launcher. One of the MoD's rare success stories – it was sourced, procured and delivered in months, rather than years or decades.

14. The awesome AC-130 Spectre gunship.

15. Australian SASR open fire from a Perentie 6x6.

16. Royal Marine sniper engaging a target during Operation Silica.

17. A Kodak moment with the US 5th Special Forces Group (Airborne).

18. Cowboy, a legendary US Special Forces operator with a 'ZZ Top' image.

19 & 20. US Special Forces on horseback shortly after 9/11.

21. Toyota pickups are a firm favourite with both the Taliban and US Special Forces. This one with some optional extras unavailable at local dealerships.

22. Members of the US 3rd Special Forces Group in a heavily laden Humvee.

23. Soldiers from the US 10th Mountain Division clear a house.

24. A soldier of the US 101st Airborne on guard duty with a SAW.

25. Soldiers of the US 101st Airborne seek out Taliban targets on a high ridge during Operation Anaconda.

26. US soldiers at Qali-e-Jhangi take cover as a JDAM slams home during a 'danger-close' air strike. Sadly, this attack was just too close – it killed and wounded several US and Northern Alliance soldiers. Also amongst the wounded were four British Special Forces operatives.

27. Looking like a scene from Star Wars, US Special Forces check-fire their weapons.

28. A US Navy SEAL checks out a suspected Taliban position.

29. Operation Mongoose: US forces clear a cave complex – always highly dangerous work.

30. Soldiers of the US 5th Special Forces Group calling in an air strike.

31. The tough and highly effective A10 Thunderbolt 11 – a welcome sight during high-tempo operations.

32. A 52H prepares to refuel over Afghanistan. Note the ordnance still available on wing hard points.

33. UAVs are playing an ever-increasing role in Afghanistan, and the UK has just ordered two MQ-9 Reapers in response to its increasing operational demands. No doubt more orders will follow.

34. Dutch Cougar and British Chinooks on the flight line at Kandahar. Of interest is the improvised armour around the cockpit of the nearest helicopter.

35. A Chinook kicking up dust at FOB Delhi during an external load re-supply mission.

36. Extraction from Operation Snake Bite.

This page and opposite top: **37, 38 & 39.** The Apache rescue mission in progress …

40. ... The Avpro Aerospace Exint pod – what British forces should have been using – makes transport far safer for passenger and crew alike. Its introduction has been raised in Parliament once already; maybe it's time to bring it up again.

41. Dawn, and the Australian SASR is on the move.

42. The brutal-looking Mastiff 6x6, minus its RPG cage protection. As yet, none are in service in Afghanistan, but four have arrived in Iraq. The comment from those who are using it – 'A great piece of kit!'

43. Taliban on patrol in a venerable pickup truck. They boldly state that they can pacify and introduce their theology to any town or village within five days of their arrival.

44. Collateral bomb damage in Afghanistan following a failed attack on a wrongly identified Al-Qaeda safe house.

45. A rare sight these days – Taliban prisoners of war.

46. Northern Alliance soldiers engage the Taliban during the Qali-e-Jhangi uprising.

47. ANA (Afghan National Army) soldiers question a local man after an RPG attack on British forces.

48. ANA soldier with AK-47 assault rifle..

49. A French Marine sniper marks out a long-range target.

50. Polish GROM Special Forces on patrol in a Toyota pickup. Maybe Jeremy Clarkson needs to do a *Top Gear* feature on these vehicles' amazing service in Afghanistan. So valuable are these pickups to the Taliban that at one time they resorted to burying them underground so as to prevent them from being attacked.

Above: **51.** Canadian soldiers receiving briefing prior to mine-clearance operations.

Right: **52.** No matter what language you speak, you will understand this sign. It does exactly what it says on the tin.

53. Canadian soldiers on patrol outside the once-impressive Kabul Palace.

54. Canadian Leopard tanks open fire on Taliban positions during the Battle of Panjwaii. It was the first time that Canada had used tanks to fire in anger for some fifty years.

55. British Para sniper team in action at Sangin.

56. Colonel Mick Ryan (no relation to the author) attending an O group prior to an operation.

57. Winning 'hearts and minds' is imperative in Afghanistan. Here, a young Afghan boy enjoys the company of a friendly Australian soldier.

58. Australian SASR walking home after a day on the ranges.

59. Afghan soldiers serving alongside the Australian army mourn a fallen comrade prior to his burial.

A-10 returning to its blast-proof pen at Bagram following a mission over Indian country.

grenade attack while repositioning the critically wounded to a third collection point. An unidentified US Navy SEAL was awarded the Navy Cross.

In addition to these awards, two members of the Australian SASR were also decorated for their part in Operation Anaconda. For outstanding bravery displayed on June 3 2004, Marine Staff Sgt Anthony Viggiani was awarded the Navy Cross, in recognition of his selfless act of charging an enemy position while wounded, in an effort to save his fellow Marines' lives.

On December 8 2004, America also recognized Canada's involvement in Operation Enduring Freedom, when it awarded two members of JTF 2 the US Presidential Unit Citation for their outstanding contribution to the multinational Special Operations Task Force in Afghanistan in 2002.

Australian soldier on night operations. For the armed forces stationed in Afghanistan, sleep is a luxury they often have to forego.

VII

Hurt Locker

When you're lying out wounded on Afghanistan's plains,
and the women come out to cut off what remains,
you roll to your rifle and blow out your brains
and go to your God like a soldier.

Rudyard Kipling

Ominous words for any soldier about to deploy to Afghanistan in the spring of 2006. But then again, why worry if you are part of the British forces? After all, the UK Defence Secretary Dr John Reid, who has just ordered your deployment, has just informed Parliament that our boys might be able to go home having done their job of helping reconstruction 'without a shot being fired'. This statement was of course a total crock: there was just no way that the British Army and its NATO Allies were going to enter Helmand Province – the Taliban's backyard – without all hell breaking loose.

The tactical planners certainly didn't believe it; they were sending in the UK's most powerful Brigade first, 16 Air Assault Brigade, equipped with the mighty Apache Helicopter gunship, Afghanistan being its first operational deployment. One can partly understand the British Government's reasons for playing this deployment down, as both the military and political situation in Iraq at the time were far from ideal. And openly admitting that the armed forces were about to be sent to hell and back wouldn't have gone down too well with the

On guard: a soldier from Germany's KSK Special Forces unit maintains a watchful eye. Note the bullet-ridden wall behind him.

The party's leadership has insisted that Germany must stay the course. 'If we leave Afghanistan now, the situation would only deteriorate,' [said] the Christian Democrats' foreign policy spokesman Eckart von Klaeden ... 'Afghanistan would be reestablished as a haven for terrorists and Islamic extremists, and we would lose all credibility in the Muslim world.' While the German Constitution, written in the wake of World War II, includes a ban on participating in any 'war of aggression,' ... [in] Afghanistan, Germany has played a larger role, leading the peacekeeping force known as ISAF, which patrols the country's north. But for the most part, it has refused to send soldiers to the restive south.

Mariah Blake, *Christian Science Monitor*, March 22, 2007

British public. Now they, the government, are paying the price for this deceit. 'Your name and your deeds were forgotten before your bones were dry. And the lie that slew you is buried under a deeper lie ...' (George Orwell).

Prior to the spring of 2006, it all seemed to be going well in Afghanistan. Both the government and the media seldom discussed it. That was of course because we were too obsessed with Iraq and its problems at the time and believed that the war in Afghanistan had already been won, back in 2002. How wrong we were.

THE NEW TALIBAN

The only reason that things were quiet was the fact that the Taliban were lying low in Helmand Province, in southern Afghanistan, learning from the mistakes that had almost gotten them wiped out after 9/11. Now, they were both better trained and better equipped than ever before and in their newfound tactical awareness had taken to heart the bitter lessons of 2002 and were more than ready for payback time.

Elsewhere in Afghanistan, things were generally good. Women could now get an education and express themselves again, kids could go to school and mums and dads could start rebuilding their lives. As for the British, well, they never left Afghanistan after 2002, they just plodded on under the umbrella of Operation Herrick, the British contribution to the NATO-led International Security Assistance Force (ISAF) and to the US-led Operation Enduring Freedom (OEF). However, in 2003, the operation started to increase in scope, its geographical responsibilities growing, in contrast to the previous year, where the numbers of British soldiers committed had dropped right down to some 300 personnel. Prior to this, there had been Operation Veritas, the British support operation to the American invasion after 9/11, which climaxed with 1,700 Royal Marines of Task Force Jacana making a sweep of east Afghanistan after Operation Anaconda. And then there was Operation Fingal, a 2,000-strong contribution and leadership of a newly formed ISAF, and the overseeing of Afghan elections.

Between 2002 and 2003, the primary component of Operation Herrick were the 300 personnel assigned to provide security in Kabul, as well as training for the new Afghan National Army (ANA). In this role, they trained the NCOs, the French trained the officers, while the Americans trained the ordinary Afghan soldier. In mid 2003, the operational strength increased to battalion level, after two provincial reconstruction teams (PRTs) were established in north Afghanistan – one at Mazar-e-Sharif, and the other at Maymana. In addition, the British provided a rapid reaction force to Maymana after riots broke out in 2006 following the Danish Muhammad cartoons controversy. In late 2003, ISAF expanded into the north, accepting overall command of the PRTs in 2004, until Sweden and Norway took over them in 2005 and 2006 respectively. This transfer of responsibility was to allow UK forces to focus on their new role in south Afghanistan. Around the same time in May 2006, Lieutenant General David Richards became the appointed commander in Kabul of NATO Headquarters Allied Command Europe Rapid Reaction Corps (ARRC) raising military forces in Kabul alone to some 1,300 infantry and signals personnel. However, as great at this commitment looked at the time, it paled into insignificance when compared to the Helmand mission.

THE HELMAND MISSION

In January 2006, Defence Secretary Dr John Reid made his momentous and now infamous announcement that the UK would commit several thousand military personnel as part of a NATO PRT in Helmand for a period of some three years. This deployment had been in the offing for quite some

A Royal Marines Field Engineering unit takes cover after a Chinese-rocket attack on their position.

Soldiers from the mighty 82nd Airborne look out for enemy activity. Of interest is the satellite navigation system.

time and formed part of ISAF's gradual mission expansion from the Kabul region to the rest of Afghanistan. The British deployment was to be coordinated with fellow NATO countries as part of a plan to relieve the predominantly American-led Operation Enduring Freedom contingent in the south. In addition, forces from both the Netherlands and Canada also deployed to Oruzgan and Kandahar respectively in an effort to maximise combat effectiveness. In support of the British were contingents from both Denmark and Estonia, who sent some 400 troops collectively. But even with these extra numbers the forces would struggle.

A Canadian armoured column slowly makes its way through the streets of Kabul, looking for combat indicators.

This is the UK's current commitment to Helmand Province, but it is subject to change. At the time of writing, there have been two troop rotations, with the next one falling due in April 2007.

Operation Herrick IV (May–November 2006):
HQ, 16 Air Assault Brigade, Household Cavalry Regiment – 1 Sqn
3rd Battalion, The Parachute Regiment
7th (Parachute) Regiment, Royal Horse Artillery – 1 Bty
9th Regiment, Army Air Corps
32 Regiment, Royal Artillery – 1 Bty
39 Regiment, Royal Engineers
23 Engineer Regiment (Air Assault), Royal Engineers – 51 Parachute Squadron
29 Regiment, Royal Logistics Corps
13 (Air Assault) Regiment, Royal Logistics Corps
7th Battalion, Royal Electrical and Mechanical Engineers
16 Close Support Medical Regiment

Operation Herrick V (November 2006–April 2007):
HQ, 3 Commando Brigade, The Light Dragoons – 1 Sqn
42 Commando, Royal Marines
45 Commando, Royal Marines
32 Regiment, Royal Artillery – 1 Bty
29 (Commando) Regiment, Royal Artillery
9th Regiment, Army Air Corps
28 Engineer Regiment, Royal Engineers
59 Independent Commando Squadron, Royal Engineers
Commando Logistics Regiment
27 Transport Regiment, Royal Logistics Corps
29 Regiment, Royal Logistics Corps
22 Field Hospital, Royal Army Medical Corps

Operation Herrick VI (April–October 2007):
HQ, 12 Mechanized Brigade, The Light Dragoons – 1 Sqn
1st Battalion, Grenadier Guards
1st Battalion, The Royal Anglian Regiment
1st Battalion, The Worcestershire and Sherwood Foresters
Regiment (29th/45th Foot)
19 Regiment, Royal Artillery
3rd Regiment, Army Air Corps
9th Regiment, Army Air Corps
4 Logistic Support Regiment, Royal Logistic Corps
4 General Support Medical Regiment

Plus special forces support: the Special Air Service (SAS), Special Boat Service (SBS), Strategic Reconnaissance Regiment (SRR) and Special Forces Support Group (SFSG).

On paper at least, it looked an impressive force, as it involved elements of all of the British spearhead and special forces. But with a resurgent Taliban to fight, plus the ever-dragging millstone of Iraq draining resources and assets at a rapid rate, there were some ravens circling that no one saw.

It all seemed to have started off well enough, when a squadron of Royal Engineers, supported by Royal Marines, built two massive fortified camps, plus a small air base for the British, NATO and Afghan forces that were to be deployed in Helmand – and encountered no resistance from the Taliban, in spite of their making numerous threats to the contrary. This was the calm before the storm. The British Forward Operations Base (FOB) in Helmand was known as Camp Bastion. It soon became a hive of activity during the spring of 2006 as soldiers worked up their skills and check-fired their weapons in anticipation of forthcoming operations. They didn't have to wait very long.

On May 1, the US Operation Enduring Freedom Task Force operating in Helmand was relieved of its command in a

Royal Marines build a PVCP for the Afghan security forces.

ceremony attended by the incoming British. Hours later, the Americans began a major offensive against the Taliban in southern Afghanistan, part of Operation Mountain Thrust. As a result of this operation, ISAF forces were now in open conflict with the Taliban. Initially all went well, but a slight setback occurred on May 24, when an RAF Hercules was destroyed in a fire soon after landing at Lashkar Gar, the capital of Helmand. Fortunately, all 27 passengers, including the British Ambassador Steven Evans, were evacuated safely. Apart from the Ambassador's near-thing, there was another interesting aspect to this aircraft's loss. It contained a number of brand new 4x4 SUVs containing millions of pounds in cash, all destined to go to local warlords as bribes for their support. Money to burn.

By June, most of the British contingent was in-country and raring to go, with 16 Air Assault Brigade providing the main thrust element. In support were 18 helicopters of the Joint Helicopter Command, comprising Chinooks, Apaches and Lynxes – these split between Kandahar and Camp Bastion. For logistics and direct combat support, they had four RAF C-130 Hercules transport aircraft and six GR7 Harriers respectively. A detachment of six aircraft of the Joint Harrier Force had already been involved prior to this in 2004, in support of OEF, out of Kandahar Airfield. It was during this operation that the RAF first sustained an aircraft loss, following a rocket attack on the airfield that completely destroyed one aircraft and damaged another.

An initial strength of some 5,700 personnel was first envisaged for Operation Herrick in 2006, with a view to stabilising at around 4,500 personnel mid-term. But following the high level of combat intensity experienced, the government reluctantly agreed to increase combat strength by an additional deployment of 1,000 troops, due to take place in 2007.

Life for any British soldier involved in direct combat operations in Helmand in the summer of 2006 was difficult – extremely difficult – as they were experiencing the most intense and sustained attacks on any British force since the Korean War. They had not just stirred up a hornets' nest – they were in it. The controversial decision to set up so-called platoon houses in certain Taliban-held areas of Helmand was made at the request of the provincial governor, who wanted an aggressive stance to be taken. And nobody in the British Army does aggression better than the Paras.

Platoon houses were little more than former police stations or government compounds that held commanding positions over a particular town or hamlet; and served to make a point. We're here – get used to it. For me, they harked back to the Boer War, where British soldiers set up blockhouses in Boer-held territory so as to disrupt the Boer lines of communication and break their psychological hold on an area. For the local Afghans, it also caused an interesting situation to develop.

'We were drunk with tiredness, but we still kept going, repelling attack after attack after attack.'

'We called it the Alamo, as we were being attacked from everywhere.'

'One of the ANP [Afghan National Police] used to be a runner for us, getting food, fags and the like. That was until the poor sod got captured and executed by the Taliban.'

3 Para at Sangin during an attack.

They were used to being dominated and controlled by the Taliban, but wanted out from under. The presence of these platoon houses meant that the Taliban were now so busy attacking them that they took their eyes off the local people, leaving them to plot their own exit strategy from the tyranny. It was a major sea change. At first they had supported the Taliban, then they had tolerated them; now, they wanted to break away. And the British were creating the perfect opportunity for this shift in attitude and loyalty. However, the Paras occupying these platoon houses were little more than sitting targets – or 'bullet magnets' – as they would say.

THE RED HOUSE

One of these Platoon houses became infamous – in the hell-hole of Sangin. For the Paras, occupying it in the summer of 2006 it was known as the 'Red House', on account of their red berets. But in recent times, the name has taken on a more

3 Para GPMG Fire Support Group in action.

'During one contact, a lad from my section fired a Jav [Javelin ATGM] at a group of tali-tubbies who were hiding among a group of trees in front of us, causing one of our full screws [full corporal] to shout at him that he was wasting Gordon Brown's money at that range. Which drew an instant response: "Fuck him – he's not here, we are."'

terrible relevance, on account of all the British soldiers who have either been killed or shed blood in its defence. As of March 2007, 10 British soldiers have lost their lives in the Red House – six Paras in the summer of 2006 alone, and four Royal Marines since, three of whom died in March 2007. It is, without doubt, the most dangerous outpost in Afghanistan.

In July 2006, it was cut off and surrounded by the Taliban, leading to a vicious and sustained series of firefights that lasted for almost five weeks. During this period there were only three days in which the Taliban failed to mount an attack.

Despite being a bloody month for both 3 Para and the Taliban, neither side broke. When news of the battle first reached the UK, there was outrage amongst the British public. Why had the Paras seemingly been abandoned? But they didn't know the half of it. Not only had the Paras had to fight off overwhelming odds during this period, in a situation reminiscent of Rorke's Drift in Natal, they had also suffered the collapse of their vital air-bridge resupply service. This was put down to serious helicopter shortages, as well as intense insurgent activity in the Sangin area. At one stage, the Paras ran out of food and were forced to forage around the local area for supplies. But that wasn't their worst problem. They discovered that at the height of this battle, the .50 calibre ammunition they were using was duff. This meant they had to to cock their .50 cal heavy machine guns each time they fired. So they could only be used for long range sniping, rather than area suppression.

What has never been explained is how this ammunition – which was of Pakistani origin – got into their supply chain without being quality checked and check-fired first. Answers on a postcard please. This crippling setback meant that all long range area suppression was down to 7.62 GPMGs within the compound, which, although respectable, were no match for the power and range of the .50.

The tactics that the Taliban were using were astute: sometimes long-range engagements, where they would use heavy 12.7mm heavy machine guns, mortars and Chinese rockets; at other times very short range engagements, where they would use assault rifles, sniper rifles, light machine guns, recoilless rifles and RPGs. When defending against the former, the Paras only had mortars, GPMGs and Javelin Anti-Tank Guided Missiles (ATGMs) immediately available. And against the latter, they fired anything that was working, basically.

It was during these engagements that the limitations of the British Army's standard-issue 5.56 mm assault rifle, the SA-80A2, became more apparent. Although an accurate and reliable weapon system, it just doesn't have the range and stopping power needed in long range firefights: hence a major current debate about its successor. Should we go back to 7.62mm, stick with 5.56mm, have a weapon that can fire both – or should we develop a new calibre? One for the boffins.

As to close air support during the defence of the Red House – sometimes it was there and sometimes it wasn't. On occasions when it was called in to suppress the Taliban, danger close warnings had to be issued to the defending Paras, as they were just as likely to sustain an injury from the ordnance as the enemy.

In modern warfare, you just do not stay in one position for long, as the enemy becomes wise to your routines and defensive limitations. So the idea of planting men in platoon houses for long periods of time seems counter-productive.

They become the hunted, and not the Taliban! In the words of Patton, 'Fixed fortifications are monuments to man's stupidity.' In fairness, the strategy was developed under the assumption that resistance levels would be relatively low and reinforcements plentiful. But alas, neither cardinal points apply. For the men defending the Red House, I have nothing but admiration, be they Paras, Marines or other; to face deadly onslaught on a daily basis over extended periods, over weeks, is a hard thing. Remarkably, they never buckled at any point.

Eventually, a relief column of American and Canadian troops arrived; and not before time. 'Nobody told us the

SLEEP DEPRIVATION

We all know what it's like to have a late night and not feel like doing much the day after. But in a combat zone, there is no such luxury. Your enemy is going to be doing his damnedest to kill you 24/7. I know of cases where officers have been so exhausted that they have given orders to their subordinates, yet had no recollection of ever doing so. Missing out on sleep for just 24 hours will lengthen your reaction times considerably; 36 hours and longer and you will feel drunk with tiredness. Even basic routines, like cleaning and stripping your personal weapon will be demanding. The higher the rank you are – the less sleep you get, as you have to look after your soldiers interests first, then take stock of the ever-changing tactical situation. You have to brief those beneath you and above you as to what is going on. All this eats into your sack time. One lesson I have always taught soldiers is to ask a specific question of their NCO or officer when awaking them from a deep sleep – especially if you need them to make a major decision. This is done to try to make sure they are awake and fully alert. Ask them, say, the registration number of their car. It is only a small thing to do, yet will potentially save lives.. In 2002 a special forces soldier called in an air strike on his own position rather than the Taliban's, killing himself and many of his colleagues. This was after days on the move without rest. Sleep deprivation is a killer.

BURN OUT

One other serious issue British soldiers in particular are facing is combat burn out. The endless cycle of back-to-back tours is leading to marriage and family breakdown at an alarming rate. This must be addressed as a matter of urgency. The British government has a simple choice. Either increase the size of the armed forces to avoid overstretch, or shape its foreign policy accordingly. Current operational demands cannot be sustained indefinitely.

Cannucks (Canadians) were coming up the road, and coz of that one nearly got slotted by a Jav. He was lucky we waited to find out who he was.'

FORKED TONGUES

Our troops will get all they need, vows Blair. It's the 4th of July, and British Prime Minister, Tony Blair has just promised British commanders in Afghanistan 'anything they need'. This promise comes after the loss of five British troops in the Red House and the deaths of two special forces personnel in the same area of Sangin all within a three-week period. He became more specific: 'When you do a mission like this, you are constantly – and so are the commanders on the ground – assessing what more we need in terms of personnel, equipment, resources. Anything they need and ask for in order to protect our troops, I'll make sure they will get.' At the same time, Britain's commander in Afghanistan, Brigadier Ed Butler, said that he *had* requested more resources, pointing out that he only had 3,300 troops in Helmand at that time, of which only 1,200 were infantry, mainly made up of Paras, Gurkhas, Fusiliers and Royal Irish Rangers. In logistical terms that equates to only 400 pairs of boots on the ground at any given time: eight hours are assigned for rest, eight for personnel admin and downtime, and eight for doing the job itself. In reality of course, that is seldom the case, as most combat soldiers do 24 hours on duty with 24 hours off. Unless you are in a platoon house, in which case, sleep will be a rare commodity.

Even with new reinforcements, the British force is woefully inadequate. The area that they are trying to protect is three times the size of Wales. As a point of comparison, there are at the time of writing 8,700 Britsh troops in Northern Ireland; and yet it is peaceful. And at the height of the Troubles some 47,000 troops were deployed there. Yet now, the British forces are fighting a vicious, tenacious enemy, in a bloody conflict that shows little sign of letting up, with barely a tenth of that number deployed in-country.

The British forces are superb at engaging the Taliban and removing them from the various places that they hide out in. But all this effort is wasted if they cannot hold that ground. As all the Taliban have to do is wait for them to go. That is exactly the situation that the Paras found themselves in during the summer of 2006, as they fought and engaged the Taliban throughout Helmand. Some did speak out at the time, such as Air Chief Marshal Sir Jock Stirrup, Britain's most senior military officer: 'There is no doubt that these two operations (Iraq and Afghanistan) are stretching us.' This drew a response from the Defence Secretary, Des Browne: 'Yes we have taken casualties, but we have overmatched the opposing forces every single time we have faced them. They have tried to block our deployment, and failed. They will continue to try to disrupt our mission – and they will fail again.' Only three weeks before, the then Defence Secretary John Reid announced that British soldiers in southern Afghanistan, '… would be happy to leave in three years' time without firing a shot.' Yes, they would have; but meanwhile back on earth, the Paras and their support unit, the Royal Irish Rangers,

COMBAT INDICATORS

There are warning signs of possible hostile action in a high-threat area. They include:

- Lack of children within villages.
- Children showing signs of extreme apprehension.
- Absence of signs of normal every day life – e.g., farmers not working their land.
- Villagers streaming out of a village.
- Abandoned villages.
- Disturbed earth on roads.
- Excessive vehicle tracks in remote areas.
- Enemy activity in unusual areas.
- Unusual vehicle movements near communication choke points.
- Suspicious filming or photographing of NATO forces.
- Change of attitude amongst normally friendly Afghans.
- Failure of normally reliable employed Afghan workers to turn up for duty.
- Unusual gatherings of Afghan locals.
- Failure of tribal leaders to offer you Chi.

were seeing life in Afghanistan as it really was. The location was the village of Zumbelay.

WHERE ARE THE CHILDREN?

Ninety minutes before, and they were all drinking tea in Camp Price, the British base at Gereshk. Now, 50 British soldiers mounted up in 15 vehicles were entering the remote village of Zumbelay. It was a 'hearts and minds' mission. Just prior to entering the village, a small fire support group (FSG) had peeled off, and headed for a ridge that overlooked the village providing a good vantage point.

The rest of the column entered the unknown. Quickly the locals came over to welcome and greet them. But unusually, there was no offer of Chi (tea) – and more alarmingly, there were no children. Children are key barometers in risk assessment in Afghanistan and Iraq. Happy children playing near you and smiling means they feel comfortable, so you can relax to a point. Nervous,

Royal Marines give covering fire from a WMIK.

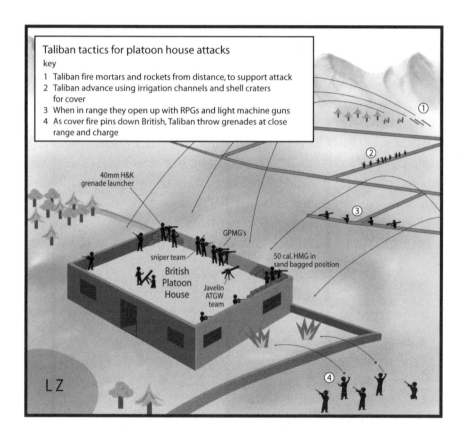

apprehensive children means that either you or someone else is making them feel uncomfortable, so you need to be on your guard. But no children means imminent danger and that you are highly likely to be attacked. The Paras and Royal Irish were.

Barely had they been ushered into the village by the local tribal leader and redirected towards a nearby bridge, when the spine chilling words of 'Contact rear' blasted over their radios, indicating that the FSG was under attack. This was a curious reversal of roles, as the FSG is there to over-watch, protect and support the main column and not the other way around. The point was academic, as bullets and RPGs were now whizzing towards both British units. And even with their GPMGs and minimis responding in kind they could not suppress the incoming fire quick enough. They therefore requested Tac-air. But there was a problem: there was none available. All the A-10 aircraft that were on close air support duty that day were already committed to another firefight nearby. That one was a higher priority: two British special forces soldiers had just been killed further north, near Sangin.

Fearing that they could be overrun, two vehicles made a break for the FSG but were driven back by RPGs and a Dushka heavy machine gun. Realising, they were in a real 'Hurt Locker' now, the Paras broke out towards a field, from which they could engage the Taliban fighters. For almost two hours, they traded fire until the welcome sound of the US A-10s was heard overhead. This gave them a chance to run for their vehicles and break-out. All lived to tell the tale, with some lessons learned. It transpired that the farmers had thought that the British had come to destroy their poppy fields – hence their co-operation with the Taliban.

This particular story illustrates the kind of Anglo-American co-operation that exists on a daily basis in Afghanistan. On this occasion, it was the Americans coming to the aid of the British. Just prior to this operation it was the Paras coming to the aid of the Americans, in Sangin, Helmand, after a ten-vehicle US convoy was ambushed by a large force of Taliban insurgents. After hearing of their plight, a 100-strong force from A Company, 3rd Battalion, the Parachute Regiment, raced to their rescue, saving a number of wounded US service personnel in the process. They did this by forming the convoy into a circle and fighting off the insurgents – just like in a hundred old cowboy films when they circled the wagons.

BRITAIN'S VIETNAM?

By September 2006, they were calling the conflict in Afghanistan Britain's Vietnam. This comparison was born as combat losses began to rocket. The loss of an RAF Nimrod MR2, near Kandahar helped to reinforce the horrible equation. All fourteen personnel on board were killed. Even though the crash was attributed to a fire caused by a fuel leak that was non combat related. It made no difference, as the British were all hurting from these mounting losses. By now, news was flowing in on an almost daily basis about the plight of our troops in Afghanistan; never the case before.

This deluge of combat stories and atrocities shocked the British public like never before. They had presumed the situation in Afghanistan to be relatively benign compared with Iraq. How wrong can you be? It was about this time that reports started to filter through of major combat operations that had taken place prior to this, in both Musa Qalah and Now Zad. Pictures of dead British soldiers being hauled across a desert plain onboard a quad bike caused great upset, as it really hammered home the truth of daily life in Helmand. These pictures were released, not by journalists, but the soldiers themselves – as they wanted the public and their loved ones to know the truth. They featured burning villages, haunted and gaunt-looking soldiers weeping over their lost friends, exhausted soldiers devoid of rest for days on end. The images blasted away the sugar-coated spin that was normally put on every story regarding the British presence in Afghanistan.

Nimrod MR2. Both night and day, this plane provides vital communication capabilities to NATO soldiers serving in Afghanistan.

British soldiers had engaged in 320 Contacts between May and September that year, firing off some 300,000 rounds of rifle and machine gun ammunition and 2,500 mortar bombs, with the loss of 11 men dead and 35 wounded.

It was during a visit to Afghanistan by General Dannatt, that the RSM of 3 Para, John Hardy, said 'Don't worry about the lads. They just want to get out there and dish it out. I feel very humble with these young lads.' He had just commented on having to bring home eleven dead men.

Those who survived had stories to tell about what what had really taken place in Helmand. Soldiers reported cases of Talibs blasting away at them while riding dirt-bikes with young children strapped to them – which placed them in an awful dilemma. Others recalled how they had gone to the aid of French special forces supporting the Afghan Army, only to find them all dead after being gutted alive by the Taliban, one of the worst atrocities of the conflict. This gruesome event goes some way to explain why the French will no longer commit troops directly in Helmand. One of the Paras later described it as being a scene from an abbatoir. As for the Paras involved in that mission, what they saw shocked them to the core. In stories of the Red House, they recalled their anger and frustration at the failure of the RAF to supply them, even citing one case where they air dropped their supplies straight into the Taliban's main defensive position in Sangin.

Perhaps the most graphic incident was in Musa Qalah. The soldiers tell how a British vehicle was destroyed by an IED, leaving several dead and wounded. As a second vehicle sped to its assistance it too was hit, this time by an RPG, causing more casualties. The Paras had to battle away trying to extract their wounded colleagues while under intense fire, making desperate use of their entrenching tools. They became aware that one of their number had been captured by the Taliban, and was being held nearby. Without hesitation, 100 of them surrounded Musa Qalah and ordered all non-combatants to leave. This done, they stormed the buildings and extracted their revenge on the Talibs holding their missing colleague. The captured soldier was eventually found but he was already dead – either from wounds sustained in the original ambush or from his captors. No Taliban insurgents left that village alive. Although no accurate casualty information is available for the Taliban, it has been estimated that some 1800 were either killed or wounded by the Paras during their tour of Afghanistan. It was a bloody period that few will ever forget.

Although great praise was heaped on all the British forces involved during this tour, from both their NATO and Afghan military Allies, one unit in particular – the Gurkhas – received considerable thanks and appreciation from the Afghan people also. This was of course on account of the way they looked – very similar to the Afghans themselves – and their ability to

Canadian soldiers on patrol in Indian country.

communicate in the same language. Two significant weapons to have when breaking down barriers.

OPERATION SILICA: RELIEF OF NOW ZAD

Following after 16 Air Assault Brigade came the Royal Marines, who lost no time in putting boots on the ground to make their presence felt. Officially they took over on October 8, 2006, but like many British units they had advance parties in-country long before to help pave the way for the main body of troops.

Barely in-country, and the Royal Marines of K Company 42 Commando are inbound by Chinook to the war-torn town of Now Zad in Northern Helmand, their mission to relieve A Company of the Royal Regiment of Fusiliers. It looks quite a nice place, says one Marine, before reading the wooden plank above one of the British defensive positions, which reads: 'ANP Hill low flying RPG's, please mind your head'. This position and the town's police station are home for the next few months. They have hardly taken in the orientation tour before someone shouts 'Contact' and a fierce firefight develops on the other side of town. No sooner has this been pacified when another breaks out, with GPMGs, .50 Cals and minimis in action. Welcome to Afghanistan.

Wanting to make an immediate impact with the local Afghans, the Royal Marines set about a number of projects. Operation Run saw the controlled destruction of a Taliban firing position known as Mud Hut, which had been targeting both British and Afghan forces. Operation Slate 1 involved some 500 Commandos securing an area near Gereshk in order to construct a series of Permanent Vehicle Check Points (PVCPs) for the use of both the Afghan police and Army. Operation Slate 2 required the building of an extra checkpoint to cover the Highway 1 route that links the provinces.

Canadian soldiers in a fierce firefight.

OPERATION BAAZ TSUKA

Operation Baaz Tsuka, or Falcon Summit as the British called it, was a Canadian forces but Royal Marine-commanded thrust against Taliban strongholds in western Kandahar Province during December 2006. In effect, it was a mini Operation Anaconda that employed the Canadians advancing from the north and east as the main attacking force, with US forces acting as a block to the south, while Royal Marines of 3 Commando Brigade blocked the west.

The focus of the operation was the village of Howz-e-Madad, on the Arghandab River, where Taliban insurgents were known to have operated out of against Afghan police and army units in the region. The operation was a complete success, in that the Taliban fled before the force arrived. Sometimes, if outgunned or out-manoeuvred, the Taliban hide their weapons in marshes or fields, and try and pass themselves off as farmers until the NATO or Afghan forces have passed. This makes them hard to identify; virtually every farmer carries a gun.

For the 2,300 Canadian troops in Afghanistan this was a proud moment, as they have borne the brunt of the fighting in Helmand, along with the British and Americans. And like the British, their casualties are mounting. They have lost 39 soldiers in Afghanistan since 2002.

THE BATTLE OF GARMSIR

In December 2006, Royal Marines of India Company 3 Commando Brigade mounted a series of operations around the war-torn district of Garmsir, the idea being to create a security footprint in the area. Roaming around in heavily armed WMIK Land Rovers, they rapidly drew attention and encouraged firefights. Their was method to this madness: once a Taliban position was positively identified, artillery or air strikes would be called in to neutralize it. This tactic worked

The U.S. military handed over a group of suspected Taliban rebels to the custody of the Afghan government ... the start of a program to transfer all Afghan prisoners it holds both in Afghanistan and Guantanamo. The 12 prisoners, captured at various times by the military since the Taliban's ouster in 2001, will be kept in a newly refurbished bloc of Pul-i-Charkhi prison on the eastern outskirts of Kabul. Afghan officials said. Taliban prisoners captured by the Afghan government have staged at least two revolts in the past in Pul-i-Charkhi and several have managed to escape from the prison.

Kabul, 3 April 2007 (Sayed Salahuddin, Reuters)

extremely well until the Taliban wised up – and started engaging the British from the homes of innocent Afghans.

The Taliban also frequently took to ambushing the Marines from the same spot – over and over again – making them susceptible to counter ambush tactics. During one patrol near the Garmsir bridge – nicknamed the bridge of doom by all who crossed it – the Marines came under sustained, accurate machine-gun and mortar fire from a mud-walled compound nearby. Despite being engaged with heavy machine-gun fire and 105mm artillery provided by 29 Commando RA, the Taliban still kept up their attack. Eventually, an air strike was called in and it took a 1000lb bomb dropped from a Dutch F-16 to finally put an end to matters.

Operating out of forward operations base (FOB) Delhi, the Commandos faced intense opposition on a daily basis, yet never faltered. However, from time to time there were setbacks. In one operation they were tasked with supporting the Afghan Army in taking control of a canal system that ran near Garmsir, in the face of heavy Taliban resistance. After days of heavy fighting in which several Afghan soldiers were killed and wounded. they took the canal – only to be told that they had to withdraw, as there were no reinforcements available.

This stuck in the craw: brave men had died, seemingly for nothing.

One other issue they had frequently to contend with was the reliability of the Afghan National Police (ANP). Unlike the Afghan Army, who are generally reliable and professional, the same cannot be said for the police. There were documented cases of them falsely claiming the sighting of Taliban in their area of responsibility to draw an immediate response from the Marines' quick reaction force (QRF). At the time, the Marines did not understand why the police were creating these fictitious reports, until one day the penny dropped and they realized that by having the Marines around the police could relax, get high on alcohol or opium, and then sleep it off. Needless to say, once they wised up to this fiddle, the Marines ran them ragged around the local district.

OPERATION CLAY

As most of us saw in the New Year with a party and a drink, M Company of 42 Commando were busy clearing villages of Taliban in and around the area of the hydroelectric Kajaki Dam in northern Helmand Province. This key critical operation involved Royal Marines and Royal Engineers tasked with providing stability and security, building a PVCP and clearing a local cave complex and insurgent training ground of explosive ordnance. The initial phase of the operation was to clear, cordon and control a 3km radius around the Dam and then expand it. The British call this the ink spot strategy, as it gradually expands and joins up with other cleared areas. It was successfully tried and tested in Malaya and Borneo and worked extremely well – but this is Afghanistan – so the jury is still out on its effectiveness here.

Major Oliver Lee, 3 Commando Brigade's Operations Officer reported: 'The operation was designed to dominate the immediate environs of Kajaki so that security could be established. 42 Commando carried out a focussed, targeted military operation intended to gain ownership of the key high ground around Kajaki. In the process of that operation we understand that their commander was killed.' During the initial operation no Commandos were killed, but scores of Taliban were. The Kajaki dam was built in 1953 by Chinese engineers and the object of the largest USAID programme in Afghanistan. Its repair will mean electricity for almost two million Afghans, plus thousands of precious jobs. So its security and protection is a top priority for NATO.

During part of the fighting Commandos fixed bayonets as they charged the Taliban positions overlooking the dam, one of which was a former Para OP codenamed Sparrowhawk. At one stage of the fighting, Taliban insurgents could be heard frantically calling for reinforcements, as they knew their number was up. After dropping a grenade in their position and clearing it, an interpreter attached to the Commandos translated the conversation: 'The Brits are coming.' 'How many?' 'I think they have sent all of them.'

To their credit, at no point did the Taliban give ground without a fight. One Royal Marine later described the action: 'I watched our red tracer zapping across the valley – it was like something from a sci-fi movie, scary, intimidating – yet fucking awesome.'

Not everything would go the Royal Marines' way. Marine Tom Curry was killed while storming a compound. The Marines have had numerous contacts since securing the Kajaki Dam and will continue to do so; the Taliban will not give up such a prize – important politically, economically and psychologically – without a struggle.

OPERATION GLACIER

In mid January 2007, ISAF troops commenced a major operation near Garmsir to clear Taliban from the area and encourage the return of Afghans driven from their homes. For the

*A US soldier from the 82nd maintains a close watch on a nearby
building as he moves through a crowd of Afghans in a village.*

An 82nd FSG looks out for Taliban activity during a sweep and clear mission.

operation to be effective, they had to take and clear a major Taliban compound known as Jugroom Fort.

Zulu Company of 45 Commando, supported by C squadron of the light Dragoons, crossed the Helmand river in their vehicles via a crossing secured by 3 Commando Brigade's Reconnaissance Force (BRF). Once across, the Marines dismounted and engaged the Taliban with small arms fire, while Apaches and fast jets provided close air support. Prior to the main assault, India Company from 3 Commando Brigade conducted a diversionary attack on the northern end of the fort, thus dividing the Taliban's fire-power.

For five hours they engaged the Taliban before withdrawing, having met ferocious fire from all sides. Lieutenant Colonel Rob MaGowan, who commanded the operation, said: 'Tremendous bravery, professionalism and endurance was evident across the battlefield by all troops involved in the operation.' This was a deliberate operation to disrupt the insurgents' freedom of movement in southern Helmand; a vital area for them to equip and move fighters into the centre of the province.

During the withdrawal phase, it was noticed that one Marine was missing, and a major rescue attempt was mounted to recover him (see *Chariots of the Damned* chapter for the full story). In Operation Glacier, Lieutenant Colonel Rory Bruce, spokesman for the British Task Force, said:

> Our intention was to show the insurgents that they are not safe anywhere, that we are able to reach out to them and attack whenever and wherever we choose, even where they think they are at their safest. To that end, the mission was a success and the insurgents now know we can and will strike at any time. By conducting operations on this basis we do not allow the Taliban to regroup and rearm during the winter period. The attack reflects UKTF's intent to restore confidence in the local population in the Garmsir area, to allow locals to improve their livelihoods without fear of prosecution from Taliban. ISAF troops are keen to restore security around the deserted town of Garmsir so that the reconstruction effort can continue and Garmsir can once again thrive as the southern gate-way to the Helmand development zone. Taliban forces have been present in the area for several months causing much of the local population to disperse. The operation sought to help provide a secure environment and reas-sure the population that they can begin to return to their homes. This will then allow ISAF to begin the process of reconstruction in the area.

During these briefings, many journalists questioned the out-come of the operation as they felt there was a suspicon that the British forces had been driven off by the Taliban. Eventually, this line of questioning drew a response from Sir Jock Stirrup: 'The UK Government line is that it was a raid, rather than an

An alert soldier from 82nd Airborne looks out for combat indicators in a seemingly calm Afghan village.

attempt to secure ground, and the primary objective was to give the Taliban a bloody nose in their own front yard.'

This of course, is just how it is at the time of writing, because neither the UK or NATO has anywhere near enough combat troops to cover an area as vast as Helmand. This obviously leaves them with no choice but to mount hit-and-run operations. This is not necessarily a bad thing: being proactive against the Taliban rather than reactive, and without huge take and hold stategies, greatly reduces the insurgents' opportunities to anticipate forthcoming operations or troop deployments.

In essence, the British conventional forces are carrying out unconventional warfare – usually the remit of special forces. This is quite an achievement, and shows that British conventional forces are more flexible in their modus operandi than others in NATO.

However, as effective as these raids are, to win a conflict, you must suppress your enemy by occupying his ground. Otherwise, he is free to exert pressure and influence on the local populace, the people the coalition forces are trying to defend.

I can fully understand the mindset of the Commandos in Helmand; they want to get out amongst the Afghan people as much as possible, both to reassure them and befriend them. That is why they are expending so much effort in building projects and programmes as a recognizable sign of change, the key to winning hearts and minds.

The Afghan people in Helmand are particularly fortunate at the moment in having so many British military engineering units deployed at this time. One of them – 131 Independent Commando Squadron (Volunteers) is a TA unit, reservists who have suspended their civilian jobs in the UK to serve out in Afghanistan as part of the regular Commando Brigades ORBAT (Order of Battle). I know them well and indeed have had the pleasure of working with them on various projects and events over the years. I can honestly say that despite their being reservists, they are amongst the most professional and hard-working soldiers I have ever met. They will, without doubt, perform a first-class job in the service of both the British forces and Afghan people. (Guys, you owe me a beer.)

More seriously, it is important that people recognize the key role that reserve forces are playing in both Afghanistan and Iraq. Without them, British armed forces in particular would seriously struggle to meet their current operational commitments. To underscore the point, I know of a young TA Para who had just completed P Company phase in 2006 – but not done his parachute course – who volunteered for service in Afghanistan and duly completed it, seeing action in some of the toughest battles of this conflict. He is typical of the sort that make up the British reserve forces; and we are lucky to have such people.

GIVE US THE TOOLS...

As is obvious from this narrative, your author is British. I would be failing in my responsibilities if, given this chance in print, I did not make the following points. We ask a lot of our people serving in Afghanistan, yet they ask little from us. It is a mark of their utter dedication and professionalism that they simply get on with the task given to them with a can-do attitude that has for the most part impressed other forces serving within NATO. Our politicians must do more to both support and equip our armed forces with the tools that they need to perform their job.

First, the snatch Land Rover, a vehicle frequently in the news, sadly for all the wrong reasons. Here is a vehicle that was designed for use in Northern Ireland, where the threat level was low, requiring it only to be armoured against petrol and blast bombs, and low-calibre rounds. And yet, our armed forces use this vehicle in both Afghanistan and Iraq on a daily basis, where it is known as a death-trap. It has contributed to the deaths of some 25 British forces personnel so far. If we were to equate this vehicle with a mode of civilian transport that was causing so many deaths, we would have the CEO of the car company in front of a court facing manslaughter and criminal negligence charges.

To be fair to the MoD, they have ordered three new types of vehicle – to complement, rather than replace – the snatch Land Rover. They are the 6x6 Vector, 6x6 Mastiff and an upgrade of the old FV432 tracked APC, called Bulldog. Great news – but where are they?

Originally, our soldiers were told that they would have at least half of these vehicles in operational service before Christmas 2006. But Santa never delivered; the forces in Iraq got four vehicles only. Which was four more than those in Afghanistan! This is totally unacceptable. Des Browne, the

On order for the British Army, the Vector PPV has yet to enter operational service.

current UK Defence Secretary, strikes me as being an honest and caring sort of person, so one would assume that he is not to blame. But somebody is – and the buck needs to stop somewhere.

All such failings have an effect on our armed forces – and on the thinking of potential recruits. At present, we have some 12,000 new recruits joining up per year – which is fantastic, considering the amount of conflicts that we are currently involved in. But it's the other figure we need to concern ourselves with: currently, around 14,000 leave the British Army per annum. It is not the conflicts themselves that are causing them to leave. It is the treatment that they get: poor housing, inadequate follow-up medical treatment and psychological support after returning home. Again, something needs to be done to address this, and quickly.

Maybe our politicians should visit the Royal Military Academy at Sandhurst for a lesson. Outside the main chapel there is a statue dedicated to the ordinary common British soldier. It is positioned there for a reason. When an officer has made his peace with God, upon leaving the chapel he sees the statue and is reminded of the fact that it is the ordinary soldier he serves, and not himself. Perhaps we need to position one outside Parliament or Number 10. Sandhurst also provides a statistic that speaks volumes abut the new pressures on British forces. Back in the 1990s, a cadet officer leaving the academy after completion of training would not deploy on an operational tour for some five years; now – it's down to four months! Our politicians need to acknowedge this and act accordingly.

In spring 2007 one British politician loftily dismissed the Royal Navy's concerns about the lack of ships and resources on the basis that Afghanistan was land locked so they were not a priority. He was obviously blithely unaware of the fact that 40% of all forces deployed in Afghanistan currently are from the Royal Navy.

I make all these point for completely valid reasons. The message needs to get out that our armed forces desperately need more manpower and assets in order to maintain the high standards that we have become accustomed to. After all, it is us that they are trying to protect.

TALIBAN TRANSFORMATIONS

We must never underestimate the Taliban. They are a resourceful and highly skilled adversary that is ever adaptable. They may be suffering right now; but there are always guns for hire in Afghanistan. Currently, a hired insurgent gets between $10 and $20 per day, depending on recruit availability within the Madrassas – or Jihad factories, as they are often called – in Pakistan. The more recruits they get, the less they pay the hired guns. The Taliban are becoming more tactically astute. Long gone are the days of big, static positions containing hundreds of fighters. Today, they fight in smaller groups, living in safe houses containing food, ammunition and spare weapons. And when things get really hot for them they scurry back over the Pakistani border for rest and recuperation; something that must be stopped. It is not just tactics that change, but also, it would seem, values. At first they were anti-drugs, now they are all for them. They condemned anybody who did not follow the Islamic faith; yet they now sometimes burn copies of the Koran when destroying Afghan schools. More recently, they have tried to pass themselves off as Mujahideen, rather than Taliban, fighters. Perhaps all these apparent changes of heart and changes of approach indicate that the coalition forces are winning against them – but just don't know it.

An alert Australian soldier on point. At the time of writing Australia has some 550 personnel serving in Afghanistan. This figure will double by 2008.

Australians on patrol during Operation Slipper.

Australian SASR 6x6 Perenties, dirt bikes and quads get checked over prior to a long-range patrol.

An Australian SASR SRV on patrol.

MILITARY OPERATIONS CONDUCTED IN AFGHANISTAN SINCE 9/11

OPERATION ACHILLES

OPERATION ANACONDA

OPERATION APOLLO

OPERATION ARCHER

OPERATION ASBURY PARK

OPERATION ATHENA

OPERATION AVALANCHE

OPERATION FALCON SUMMIT

OPERATION HAVEN DENIAL

OPERATION HEADSTRONG

OPERATION HERRICK (CODENAME OF BRITISH OPERATION IN AFGHANISTAN)

OPERATION LIGHTNING RESOLVE

OPERATION MEDUSA

OPERATION MOUNTAIN FURY

OPERATION MOUNTAIN LION

OPERATION NIBIO

OPERATION NORTHERN WIND

BATTLE OF PANJWAII

OPERATION PTARMIGAN

OPERATION RESOLVE

OPERATION SLIPPER

OPERATION SNIPE

OPERATION SPARVIERO

OPERATION THRUST

BATTLE OF TORA BORA

OPERATION VERITAS

OPERATION VIPER

OPERATION VOLCANO

OPERATION WARRIOR SWEEP

The amphibious all-terrain Viking. British forces are the first in the world to use the vehicle. 'We still have the odd moan about kit ... but we have no complaints with this vehicle. It's hoofin.' (RM Michael Robertson.)

TALK THE TALK

As from mid 2007 all Army Officer cadets attending the Royal Military Academy Sandhurst will be taught Arabic as part of their training course.

Learning Arabic makes good sense, as a considerable part of the British Armed Forces are deployed in this part of the world. Conversing in a local language is of course good for winning hearts and minds as it helps to create trust and confidence in the troops.

Australian troops assist Afghan locals, towing their tractor with a Bushmaster.

Conclusion

As I write these final pages, British, American, Canadian, Dutch, Danish and Afghan forces have just commenced Operation Achilles, a major spring offensive against the Taliban in Helmand Province. Its ultimate aim is to drive them out of this region and back into Pakistan. It will be, without doubt, one of the greatest challenges that NATO forces have had to face in Afghanistan and it is one that they cannot afford to fail.

Already, four members of the Royal Marines involved in this operation have been killed in action, along with scores of Taliban fighters – and this in only the first week. For both sides it is a key battle; neither can afford to lose control of Helmand. Assuming NATO wins and does force the Taliban out of Helmand and back into Pakistan, then it will be a major victory. But it will not be the end of the Taliban, nor the end of the conflict: they then have to be kept there. That's where the next phase begins, involving Pakistan like never before. They will have the unenviable task of sealing the border and containing the Taliban within. Pakistan's President, General Pervez Musharaff, has pledged to commit some 80,000 border police and soldiers to this task; but even that number, in my opinion, is insufficient. The border is just to long and porous for that level of policing to be effective. He has also offered to both fence and mine it; but this option could be counter-productive as it could cause casualties to innocent Afghan refugees fleeing the conflict, thereby driving them into the arms of the Taliban.

There is a logical supposition one could make that Pakistan does not want the border control to be too efficient for its own reasons, which are not being discussed. One reason, and the most important, is that the Pakistani government is seriously concerned about the possibility of Taliban influence expanding more and more within its territory – beyond the Quetta border area. They fear a Taliban State will develop in Pakistan, leading to the possibility of serious internal conflict. To my eyes such a state within a state is already in existence. At the same time, President Karzai of Afghanistan accused Pakistan at the end of 2006 of trying to turn his people into 'slaves' by equipping the Taliban. The Pakistani positions are mutually contradictory. They can't both be true.

As for NATO, they are going to be in Afghanistan for a very long time to come. And assuming all goes well, their role will switch from direct conflict to reconstruction and security but that's clearly only going to be after some very serious fighting is done. The most troubling thing is that I do not think that we have seen the worst of it yet. I do believe that we will prevail in the long run. But it will be, in the words of Wellington, 'the most desperate business.'

The Taliban commander Mullah Dadullah yesterday vowed to continue kidnapping foreign reporters following the release of his brother and four other senior militants in exchange for a kidnapped Italian journalist [Daniele Mastrogiacomo of *La Repubblica*] ... The Taliban beheaded Mastrogiacomo's driver, Syed Agha, in an apparent ploy to accelerate negotiations. There is still no sign of his translator, Ajmal Naskhbandi, a Kabul-based journalist.

The Guardian, London, 23 March 2007

The Fallen

Dedicated to the memory of all the brave men and women of NATO and the Afghan security forces who have given their today, for Afghanistan's tomorrow.

As of 12 March 2007, a total of 53 British Forces personnel have died while serving in Afghanistan since the start of operations in November 2001.

Of these, 31 are classed as Killed in Action or Died of Wounds sustained from Action (28 are classed as Killed in Action, 2 are classed as Died of Wounds sustained from Action).

22 are known to have died either as a result of illness, non-combat sustained injuries or accidents, or have not yet officially been assigned a cause of death pending the outcome of an investigation.

UK ROLL OF HONOUR

Private Chris Gray, 1st Battalion Anglian Regiment, aged 19, from Leicester.

WO2 Michael Smith, 29 Commando Regiment Royal Artillery, aged 39, from Liverpool.

Marine Benjamin Reddy, 42 Commando Royal Marines, aged 22, from Ascot in Berkshire.

Lance Bombardier Ross Clark, aged 25, from South Africa, and Lance Bombardier Liam McLaughlin, aged 21, from Lancashire.

Marine Scott Summers, 42 Commando Royal Marines, aged 23, from Crawley, East Sussex.

Marine Jonathan Holland, 45 Commando Royal Marines, aged 23, from Chorley in Lancashire.

Lance Corporal Matthew Ford, 45 Commando Royal Marines, aged 30, from Immingham, Lincolnshire.

Marine Thomas Curry, 42 Commando Royal Marines, aged 21, from East London.
Lance Bombardier James Dwyer, 29 Commando Regiment Royal Artillery, aged 22.

Marine Richard J Watson, 42 Commando Royal Marines, from Caterham, Surrey.

Marine Jonathan Wigley, 45 Commando Royal Marines, aged 21, from Melton Mowbray, Leicestershire.

Marine Gary Wright, 45 Commando Royal Marines, aged 22, from Glasgow.

Lance Corporal Paul Muirhead, 1 Royal Irish Regiment, aged 29, from Bearley, Warwickshire.

Lance Corporal Luke McCulloch, 1 Royal Irish Regiment, aged 21.

Corporal Mark William Wright, 3rd Battalion, The Parachute Regiment, aged 27, from Edinburgh.

Private Craig O'Donnell, The Argyll and Sutherland Highlanders, 5th Battalion The Royal Regiment of Scotland, aged 24, from Clydebank.

The following fourteen personnel were killed following the crash of a Nimrod MR2 aircraft on Saturday 2 September 2006. They were:

Flight Lieutenant Steven Johnson, aged 38, from Collingham, Nottingham.
Flight Lieutenant Leigh Anthony Mitchelmore, aged 28, from Bournemouth.
Flight Lieutenant Gareth Rodney Nicholas, aged 40, from Redruth, Cornwall.
Flight Lieutenant Allan James Squires, aged 39, from Clatterbridge.
Flight Lieutenant Steven Swarbrick, aged 28, from Liverpool.
Flight Sergeant Gary Wayne Andrews, aged 48, from Tankerton in Kent.
Flight Sergeant Stephen Beattie, aged 42, from Dundee.
Flight Sergeant Gerard Martin Bell, aged 48, from Ely, Cambridgeshire.
Flight Sergeant Adrian Davies, aged 49, from Amersham, Bucks.
Sergeant Benjamin James Knight aged 25, from Bridgewater.
Sergeant John Joseph Langton, aged 29, from Liverpool.
Sergeant Gary Paul Quilliam, aged 42, from Manchester.
Corporal Oliver Simon Dicketts, The Parachute Regiment.
Marine Joseph David Windall, Royal Marines, aged 22.

Ranger Anare Draiva, 1 Royal Irish Regiment, aged 27, from Fiji.

Lance Corporal Jonathan Peter Hetherington, 14 Signal Regiment (Electronic Warfare), aged 20 from South Wales.

Corporal Bryan James Budd, 3rd Battalion The Parachute Regiment, aged 29, from Ripon.

Lance Corporal Sean Tansey, The Life Guards, aged 26, from Washington, Tyne and Wear.

Private Leigh Reeves, Royal Logistic Corps, aged 25, from Leicester.

Private Andrew Barrie Cutts, Air Assault Support Regiment, Royal Logistic Corps, aged 19, from Mansfield.

Captain Alex Eida, Royal Horse Artillery, aged 29, from Surrey.

Second Lieutenant Ralph Johnson, Household Cavalry Regiment, aged 24, from Windsor.

Lance Corporal Ross Nicholls, Blues and Royals, aged 27, from Edinburgh.

Private Damien Jackson, 3rd Battalion The Parachute Regiment, aged 19, from South Shields, Tyne and Wear.

Corporal Peter Thorpe, Royal Signals, aged 27, from Barrow-in-Furness, Cumbria, and Lance Corporal Jabron Hashmi, Intelligence Corps, aged 24, from Birmingham.

Captain David Patten, The Parachute Regiment, aged 39.

Sergeant Paul Bartlett, Royal Marines, aged 35.

Captain Jim Philippson, 7 Parachute Regiment Royal Horse Artillery, aged 29, from St Albans in Hertfordshire.

Lance Corporal Peter Edward Craddock, 1st Battalion The Royal Gloucestershire, Berkshire and Wiltshire Regiment.

Corporal Mark Cridge, 7 Signal Regiment, aged 25.

Lance Corporal Steven Sherwood, 1st Battalion, The Royal Gloucestershire, Berkshire and Wiltshire Light Infantry, aged 23, from Ross-on-Wye, Herefordshire.

Private Jonathan Kitulagoda, The Rifle Volunteers, aged 23, from Plymouth.

Sergeant Robert Busuttil and Corporal John Gregory, Royal Logistic Corps.

Private Darren John George, The Royal Anglian Regiment.

MILITARY FATALITIES IN AFGHANISTAN BY COUNTRY

AFGHAN SECURITY FORCES	1,500 (Estimated)
AUSTRALIA	1
CANADA	51
DENMARK	3
FRANCE	9
GERMANY	18
ITALY	9
NETHERLANDS	4
NORWAY	1
PORTUGAL	1
ROMANIA	4
SOUTH KOREA	1
SPAIN	20
SWEDEN	2
UK	53
USA	376

US Helicopter losses for Afghanistan and Iraq since 9/11 currently stand at 130 – of which a third were shot down.

NON-MILITARY CASUALTIES (ESTIMATED)

AFGHAN CIVILIANS	7,500
NORTHERN ALLIANCE	200
AL-QAEDA	1,500
TALIBAN	7,000

US NAVY SEALS
TALIBAN TOUR

Index